Loving
Through
Thick and Thin

Loving Through Thick and Thin

ESSENTIALS FOR A HEALTHY, THRIVING, AND SEX-FILLED RELATIONSHIP

Debra Foxx

Cover designed by Mario G. Sequeira

ISBN: 978-0692303764
ISBN 10: 0692303766

I dedicate this book to my darling husband, the love of my life, Edwin "Fuji" Martinez. In you I've found the perfect partner, companion, and soul mate. Your endless love, committed support, and faithful words of encouragement give me the strength I need to accomplish anything. Thank you for always being my rock and my number one fan. Thank you for loving me the way that you do—unconditionally. I couldn't be or do any of this without you. I love you more than you can possibly conceive. Thanks for not getting off the train and I'm still several laps ahead of you (smile).

Love always,

Your Queen Bee

Foreword

She had me at sex-filled relationships, but this isn't about me.

Debra Foxx has written a light-hearted, witty yet brutally honest book that offers readers the essentials on the things most of us want most: healthy, thriving and the aforementioned, sex-filled relationships.

Debra is qualified, not because she and her husband have the kind of relationship she writes about but because she and her husband have worked together, fought together and loved together to make it so.

What I like most about "Loving Through Thick and Thin" is Debra's transparency on what it takes to build a strong relationship. Her story is personal and poignant, raw and relatable, engaging and empowering. Best of all, it includes practical tools that we all can incorporate into our current relationships or the relationship we'll have in the future if we've somehow blown our last one.

Career changes, financial struggles, and personal dissatisfaction are some things most of us have experienced. Debra reminds us that there is a way out but it takes more than just wanting it. It takes wanting it enough to make changes that begin knowing who we are and what we need. After that's been figured out, we have to be willing to make sacrifices for the people closest to us.

I've had the pleasure of seeing Debra and her family in action. There is no doubt in my mind they stand firmly together on the foundation laid out in "Loving Through Thick and Thin" that includes: faith, laughter, commitment, mutual respect, accountability and passion.

Whether I'm sharing the stage with Debra and listening to her motivate audiences with her empowering messages or chatting with her about balancing work, life and family, I'm touched by her openness and willingness to share her story. It is a testament of her giving spirit and why I'm happy to encourage you to read this book.

Getting her personal story from the heart to the page was no easy journey. As an author, speaker, entrepreneur and mom, I know how she labored over this project and I'm so proud of her for seeing it through.

But if you're expecting all the answers to a happy marriage you should know this isn't her style. Debra readily admits that she's a work in progress and so are all of our relationships.

Loving is an action word and "Loving Through Thick and Thin" shares the truth about the ongoing process that changes and grows as much as we do, but only if we're willing to do the work. When we care about a project we're willing to buy the tools we need. It should be true of our relationships as well and "Loving Through Thick and Thin" by Debra Foxx is one of the first tools to invest in.

Nikki Woods
Global Visibility Expert &
Senior Producer of the
Tom Joyner Morning Show

Acknowledgments

First and foremost, without God this would not be possible and for that I give him all the praise and the glory. I thank Him for blessing my union the way he has that I may share a small glimpse of what it is I'm always so grateful for. Most importantly I thank Him for always being present through our thick and thin.

With special thanks:

To my two beautiful sons, Christian and Zachary. I love you both more than you could possibly imagine. One day when you have kids of your own you will understand what that means. I know working on this book took me away from you many nights, but I promise it was not in vain but a mere sacrifice. I hope I've made you proud.

To the best parents in the world, Garth and Beverly Sequeira. Thank you for supporting the dream even though it was contrary to what you'd envisioned for my life. Your forty plus year union has been a great example for Fuj and I. Words cannot express my sincere gratitude Mom and Dad. I will never be able to repay all that you have done for me but I promise I will die trying.

Thank you Dean, Ray, and Mario. You guys are the best brothers a girl could ever hope for. Even though I'm the middle child and the only girl, I'm STILL the boss (and the favorite—LOL). I've always felt protected and loved by you. Mario thank you for designing such a stellar book cover, you rock! So happy you were a part of the book in that way.

A big thank you to my cousin Janice Sequeira. From spending summers in New York until now, we've always had a special bond. I know I fought you tooth and nail on pursuing this dream; now I can't thank you enough. I remember that conversation as if it happened yesterday. Thanks for not giving up and being so stubborn in your pursuit. Not only do you believe in me but you've always believed in the love Fuj and I share, thank you. Now, like you, I believe.

Thank you to all of the following for being a part of the Debbie/Fuj journey since forever: my in-laws, the Martinez Family, my cousins Nadine and Sophia, Aunty P., Uncle Carol, The Sheppard Girls, The Guilers, and Kim G. Your support has not gone unnoticed over the years.

Thank you Carol C. Bailey for all of your perfectly timed prayer-filled phone calls and text messages. I've claimed and received each and every one of them.

A huge thank you to all the contributors of "101 Tips for a Successful Marriage," and the #itsthesmallthings segment of the book. Thank you for trusting me with your stories. I'm certain readers will find them inspiring and valuable.

A special thank you to the following women for putting up with my constant rants and moments of insanity while writing this book. Not once did you ever display signs of frustration or that you were tired of hearing about it. Instead, you encouraged me to push through. Climbing this mountain was a tough task and it's because of you I've reached the top. I love and appreciate this cheering squad: Roxanne Ward, Sinita Wells, Michelle Campbell, Madge Geohagen, Donna Wilson, and Michelle Bartley.

To my Grandma Edith. You've always been a fan of Fuj and I wish you could be here to celebrate this milestone. I know you're watching with pride-filled eyes. I miss and love you so very much.

Last but definitely not least, Aprille Franks-Hunt. You are simply amazing! You are a beast when it comes to pushing someone beyond what they *think* they are capable of accomplishing. I'm now doing things I never thought I could do or had the guts to. Who knew that a friendship that began on Facebook in 2011 would have blossomed into true, genuine, authentic sisterhood. Your no non-sense "ain't nobody got time for that" attitude was at times irksome but in the end it was exactly what I needed. Thanks for investing not only your time, but your knowledge into me and the Debra Foxx brand. Like most, you too believed and I thank you.

It's simply impossible to list my countless number of supporters, friends, and family members that has played a significant role on my journey and for that my sincere apologies. If you've shared a word of encouragement, purchased a copy of this book, prayed for me, helped and supported in anyway, from the bottom of my heart *I thank you.*

Lots of Love,
Debra

Table of Contents

Chapter 1 – Why "Drop Those Panties"
Was My First choice 1

Chapter 2 – Love At First Sight—Well,
Maybe Not So Much 7

Chapter 3 – Our Lives As Newlyweds 21

Chapter 4 – Surviving Our First Tragic
Loss together 31

Chapter 5 – My Professional Challenges
While Chasing the Dream 37

Chapter 6 – Losing Everything...
Just About! 49

Chapter 7 – What Drives Me to Succeed 61

Chapter 8 – How We've Kept It Hot
and Steamy 73

Chapter 9 – #ITSTHESMALLTHINGS 83

PART TWO — TESTIMONIALS, ESSENTIALS, AND WORKBOOK 97

Chapter 10 – What Makes a Relationship Successful 99

Chapter 11 – Respect: If You Want it, You've Got To Give It 109

Chapter 12 – Trusting Your Spouse or Your mate 115

Chapter 13 – Without Communication Your Relationship Can Perish 123

Chapter 14 – The Importance of Sex to a Marriage 131

Chapter 15 – 101 Tips for a Successful Relationship 139

Endnotes 157

About The Author

Actress, author, and host, Debra Foxx is driven by all facets of her life. She's committed to not only pursuing her dreams and greatest desires, but to encourage and motivate others into knowing that they are just as capable of doing the same. Her drive and determination is admirable and is encouraging to those who are fortunate to know her.

Through both her book and her blog, Debra's Daily Dose, she is able to share her thoughts, ideas, and creativity, on numerous topics. In particular:

∿ *Relationships,* based on and surrounding her twenty year plus love affair with her loving and supportive husband. Her eBook: "*5 Key Components to a Successful Relationship,*" has been widely received by viewers and followers.

∿ *Success,* she was brave enough to leave Corporate America to purse her dreams as an entertainer. In a very short time Debra has found tremendous success in the roller coaster industry of entertainment.

∿ *Motivation & Encouragement,* she believes without it she would never have made it as far as she has and feels the need to pay it forward.

Debra has lead and played the leadership role for years through her own women's organization, the lead host of an online talk show, and for the past two years as an instructor where she speaks to young girls on a topic that they often struggle with, thanks to society's belief and perception, *Body Image & First Impression.* She has truly perfected teaching this class to those who suffer from low self-esteem, lack of confidence, and loving themselves. For Debra, being in front of the mass is a very comfortable place for her.

Debra's mantra, *dream, then believe* is a derivative of one of her favorite quotes, "your dreams are what you were meant to be, what you are is what you settled for."

Follow On All Social Media Forums:
@DebraFoxx

Twitter, Facebook, Instagram, Pinterest, LinkedIn

Would also like to mention my blog:

www.DebrasDailyDose.com

Part One

LIFE'S JOURNEY

CHAPTER 1

Why "Drop Those Panties" Was My First Choice

You have a lifetime to enjoy one another. Don't waste a day of it.

~ James Dobson

On March 15, 2014, at a conference called the "Fabulous New You" in Oklahoma City, Oklahoma, I was a guest panelist on the topic of success. The keynote speaker at the conference was Tisha Campbell-Martin, actress, singer, and author. She's well-known for her roles in the hit sitcoms *Martin* and *My Wife and Kids*.

Tisha spoke about a number of things in her thirty-minute spiel, but what made her smile and

1

act like a giddy high school girl was when she spoke about the love of her life, her husband and fellow actor Duane Martin. Already, Tisha had a great big smile that could brighten any room, but something about her smile and her body language was different when she spoke about her husband, and *I got it!* I can completely relate because I feel the same way when I talk about my husband, the love of my life. She spoke about the two of them being a team, raising their kids together, etc., but what was most memorable was when she said something to the tune of "ladies, I know you're tired when you get home from work, you're doing everything in the house, you're taking care of the kids…but when your man comes home, you need to drop it!" Without hesitation, in almost an out-of-body experience or a hallelujah moment, I blurted out, *"Yes! "Drop those panties!* With a great big smile, Tisha looked over at me and said, "Oooh, what did you just say, young lady?" The audience erupted into laughter as I proudly and boldly repeated the words *"Drop those panties!"* Really and truly, I wanted to jump up on the stage and high-five Tisha, as I agreed with her 1,000 percent. The lady behind me looked at me and shook her head no and said, "I'm just too tired." I thought to myself, "This is why we have so many unhappy marriages around the world, not just here in the States." Soon after, the chaos settled, and Tisha spoke for a little while longer and then concluded with a heartfelt closing, finally exiting the stage. The conference was a huge success but, like everything else, all good things must come to an end.

The next day began with brunch at KD's. There were about twelve of us at this chic hot spot. If you're ever in OKC, be sure to stop by, you'll love it. We were still on an emotional high from all that occurred the day before, myself included. Brunch felt like an extension of the conference. The partying and celebration continued at KD's. It was all we could talk about. About two hours later we began to say our good-byes, as some folks had early-afternoon flights. I had an evening flight, so I still had time to socialize and get some more laughter in. We left KD's and made our way over to The Body Wrap Spalon, (intentionally spelled spa-lon) owned by Tiffany Lenox Miller, who was also on the success panel. Tiffany and her team invited us inside to be a part of their afternoon motivational round table. It was unique to me; however, I understood the importance of how this ritual helped get their day started. For approximately two hours, twelve of us sat around a table and simply talked about a number of things, including the conference. We were there long enough to work up an appetite and eat again after having left KD's. Before it came to an end, something was said in reference to relationships, and in one breath, sitting at the edge of my chair, I said, "Let me shut this down now. I've been with my man some twenty-plus years, and do you know that when he sends me a text saying 'I'm heading home,' I get hot and bothered and an entire plan of action goes into place, from taking a bath to doing my hair, basically getting ready for him. Why? Because I am *in love* with him. I don't just love him. Just thought I would put that out there." Without hesitation, friend Shalena said, "That's right, girl, and that should be the name of your book: *Drop Those Panties!*" To which I responded, "You know it, and great point." It was at that very moment I felt and heard the wheels turning in my head. It's been on my heart to write this book for years, but I wasn't ready and was intimidated by the entire process. If I got a dollar every time someone told me to write this book over the years about my relationship, about our love, I would have been a millionaire by now, but it wasn't until that moment that I felt compelled to do so.

In no way, shape, or form am I claiming any of the following: that I am perfect, that my relationship is perfect, that I have a degree in psychology, or that I'm a licensed counselor. None of the above. What I am is a woman who is truly in love with her husband after two-plus decades, and I'd simply like to share some of the reasons why I think our relationship works. From this book I hope you will find strength and encouragement to make some adjustments to your own relationship. It hurts my heart to see other couples feeling stuck, just waiting for the days to pass, not really excited about who they are with, waiting for the kids to graduate from high school and go off to college so they can do the inevitable: file for a divorce. Here's a disheartening fact: *"50 percent of first marriages, 67 percent of second, and 74 percent of third marriages end in divorce,"* according to Jennifer Baker of the Forest Institute of Professional Psychology in Springfield, Missouri. That really does break my heart.

I would like nothing more than for people to feel or experience even a small fraction of what I'm speaking about. I want to be in the company of other couples who are madly in love with their spouses or soul mates. If you think loving and being in love with your spouse are the same thing, I'm confidently saying no, they are not. This is only my opinion, and I am entitled to it. I feel like loving someone is easier to do than being in love with that person. Trust me, I get it. Most of the couples I know love their spouses but are not "in love" with them, and they think it's totally fine. If it works for them, fantastic. I'm simply saying being in love is extremely distinct than simply loving someone. It takes work, and it makes a tremendous amount of difference in the relationship. If you are not willing to put in the work and make the sacrifice, then you're settling for mediocrity.

Journal Entry—October 14, 2013

Today is Columbus Day and Fuji has it off. We started off by making love – always a great way to start your day. After that we just went to a few different stores. It was something so simple but we loved it. We spent time together just people watching in Winter Park then having lunch at PF Changs. Before we knew it, it was time to pick up Zachary from school. The weather was perfect and Fuj and I had a super day. He is such a great man and most importantly he believes in me.

Interesting Fact: No sex in a marriage has a much more powerful negative impact on a marriage than good sex has a positive impact.

CHAPTER 2

Love At First Sight—Well, Maybe Not So Much

Happily ever after is not a fairy tale. It's a choice.

~ *Fawn Weaver*

Way back in 1983, Miami, Florida, who knew that this little big-haired, brown-eyed, tall, lanky Jamaican island girl would meet the love of her life at the age of twelve? It was the seventh grade. I remember all the budding teenage girls talking about the boys they thought were cute and whom they liked. There were a few; however, there was one boy in particular, Edwin Martinez, also known as Fuji. FYI,

I will be interchanging both names throughout the book. Before you ask, Edwin was given that nickname as a child by his parents. One of his father's favorite television show was McHale's Navy and his favorite character was Fuji Kobiaji, played by Japanese actor Yoshio James Yoda. Fuji was born in Miami, Florida, but his parents and most of his family are from Puerto Rico. Like me, Fuji was tall and skinny, with gorgeous brown eyes, green if the sun caught them just right. One day after school, I can clearly remember my friends saying, "Fuji is so sweet and cute," and I remember thinking and even saying, "He's not all that." They raved about his eyes and his smile. To me he had nothing on my true first crush, whom we will call Jerry. My friends even spoke about the way Fuji dressed. In the mid '80s, MC Hammer was a huge icon. He was famous for his fancy footwork and his sense of style. Often he wore what we called "parachute pants." The name suggests it all. Fuji wore parachute pants all the time with dress shoes, and at that age that was "swag," or at least so he thought. I was annoyed and not impressed by his so-called swag at all. Even today, I don't think he is convinced that I felt that way, but it's the truth.

Fast-forward two years to 1985, ninth grade, celebrating my fourteenth birthday. Growing up I had a birthday party every year until I was eighteen, so that year was no different. I was the only girl of four children, and a daddy's girl, too, so you already know what that means. Anyway, I remember inviting the boy I really liked, Jerry, to my birthday party. He never came because he was grounded—idiot! So who came instead? Fuji and his posse of two—it might have been three. I was annoyed by them showing up. I don't think they were even invited, but they showed up anyway, and I was irritated. So there we were having a good time, girls in one corner snickering and being silly girls, boys in the other corner ignoring the girls—boys being boys. When it was time to cut the cake, I asked my friends who they thought the cutest boy was and who I should cut the cake with, and overwhelmingly they said, "Fuji!" I sighed, rolled my eyes, and reluctantly said, "OK, I guess," and so we cut the cake. An hour or so had gone by and it was time to dance to some of our favorite songs, such as "Rhythm of the Night," by DeBarge, "Nightshift," by the Commodores, and "Oh Sheila," by Ready for the World. It's funny how your mind remembers certain details about specific events over the course of your life. My cousin and my dad were disc jockeys at my party, and I remember them mixing Chaka Khan's "I Feel for You" and "Saving All My Love," by Whitney Houston. Why did they mix those two songs? That's another story, but if it makes you feel better, their lives as DJs were short lived and their true professions are car mechanics. Anyway, some of us coupled up and started dancing. While Fuji and I were dancing, he was trying to be smooth, I guess, and began whispering in my ear, nothing of which I heard because Dad had these larger-than-life speaker boxes blasting loud enough for the entire block to hear. Despite not being able to hear him, I thought it was cute and was flattered by all of the attention I was suddenly getting from him. Did he think I was cute? That's pretty much all I remember about that birthday party.

The following Monday at school he began meeting me at the end of my classes and walking me to the next. He carried my books, opened doors, and it always ended with an innocent kiss on the cheek at the last class—chivalry is so dead today. This innocent wooing went on for about two and a half months. He made me feel special. He never called me names or made me feel "less than." Everyone said we made a cute couple because we were the same height (tallest of all our friends) and we both had those gorgeous brown eyes. (Sigh.) All was great until the "new" girl came to school, and that was the end of that courtship. The "new" girl had a great figure and was plump in all the right areas. In addition, she was cute, stylish, and had a great head of hair. She was all the things I was not at the age of fourteen. At fourteen, I was so awkward in my own skin. I was so thin I would turn sideways and disappear. The boys made it very clear that my lack of curves was not attractive. They made fun of my full lips and bright, big smile. If only they knew I was blossoming into my money-maker. None of my girlfriends looked like me. They all had maturing breasts, a cute butt, or worse— both. I had neither! Secretly I wished I had their bodies, and I felt this way for many years. Needless to say I was heartbroken over the end of our courting. For the next four years of high school, my love, or should I say very strong like, for Fuji went unnoticed and ignored by him. My poor best friend Kim was probably sick of hearing me talk about him all the time.

What I felt for Fuji was undeniable. He had a girlfriend, or two (possibly three or four), during the remaining years of high school. There were other guys that I liked, but none quite like him. My first serious boyfriend came along right after graduating from high school, and that relationship lasted a year and a half. Shockingly, this boyfriend was Jerry. He was the one who was grounded and was not able to attend my fourteenth birthday party. He was the one I had a major crush on in the seventh grade. He was Fuji's buddy in elementary school; an interesting fact I learned later once Fuji and I started dating. Like Fuji, Jerry was also of Puerto Rican descent. He was born in New York, but his parents and other relatives were from Puerto Rico. My attraction toward Puerto Ricans began in the seventh grade. My girlfriends and I were simply drawn to this small Hispanic community of boys. Their jet-black hair, caramel skin, and smooth demeanor was eye catching. Might I add, they were equally attracted to us.

The first six months with Jerry were great. Like most couples, we had fun together and spent a lot of time with each other. Jerry, however, was a high school dropout and already had a child by the time he was eighteen—two facts I knew my parents would not have been pleased with, especially my Dad. Even though my parents never actually sat down and spoke to us about what types of spouses they wanted us to have, it was always implied; part of the Jamaican culture, I guess. The implication: they must be educated, no kids, great job, and able to provide for the family. This held true for my siblings and most of my cousins as well. While dating Jerry, I started to pursue modeling seriously. I entered competitions, submitted my pictures, and even had a few photo shoots. Initially, Jerry supported it and, I thought, loved the idea that his girlfriend was a model. We would go shopping and together select outfits that complemented my five-foot-ten-inch,

105-pound modelesque frame. I hated being so thin and didn't particularly enjoy shopping. I would drink gallons of milk to try to gain weight, but that never worked. I was far from loving my body but had no choice but to work with what I had.

Seven months in and the relationship was no longer what it used to be. Jerry was now displaying signs of jealousy. The very outfits that we shopped for together were no longer appropriate for me to wear with or without him. Initially I thought nothing of it but quickly learned I hated being controlled and treated like a child. He often accused me of doing things that I was not doing. In many ways this relationship made me mad, angry, bitter, paranoid, and, worst of all, self-conscious about my body. A year later I decided I'd had enough and wanted out of this toxic relationship. Nothing about my relationship with Jerry was healthy or showed signs of the type of life I wanted to live, so I ended it in the summer of 1991.

Shortly after ending it with Jerry, I was hired as the intermission performer for an upcoming fashion show. Fuji's sister was a participant, so I knew he would be attending. I thought his girlfriend at the time would have accompanied him to the show as well, but she didn't. Over the years Fuji and I innocently flirted with each other, but nothing evolved through our flirting until this very night. As the performer, I knew I would be wearing some of the hottest pieces of fashion by notable designers in the show. Once I realized Fuji's girlfriend was not present and I no longer had a boyfriend, the flirting was in full swing. The ball would be in his corner and he could do with it what he chose.

The fashion show was a success, his sister was first runner-up, it ended, and all went their separate ways except Fuji and me. He had recently bought a new car and asked if I wanted to go for a spin, and without hesitation I said, "Yes, why not?" That spin ended at Denny's, where I ordered the fancy-schmancy shrimp dinner. Would you believe I ate only two, at most three, of the two dozen shrimps because I was trying to be cute and didn't want to look like an idiot eating in front of him? Ladies, you know what I mean. He had no problem chomping down all of his food. Why do we do that as girls? Later it was impossible to disguise the affair my tummy was having with my ribs due to lack of food!

When dinner was over, it was time to take me back to the hotel where the fashion show was held, so that I could get my car. I stalled as long as I could, having silly conversations about anything just so he wouldn't leave. It was hard to remain calm and unaffected by the six-foot charmer that I had liked since the ninth grade. I couldn't let him know how very much I wanted to be his girlfriend and how terribly magnetized by him I was. Once we were back at the hotel he offered to follow me home to ensure that I made it home safely. First of all, I was at most, fifteen minutes away from home and did not need or require an escort, but why would I turn that offer down? I didn't—I didn't want the night to end. On my way I cleverly adjusted the mirror, fluffed my hair, tweaked my makeup, and took a minor detour to a nearby park; he followed. I got out of my car and into his. We hung out for about fifteen minutes, again talking about anything. Finally, the night ended just as I'd hoped: with us exchanging phone numbers and a nice, long kiss good-night.

Fuji and I spent the next few months genuinely getting to know each other. We spent so much time together it was difficult to ignore the chemistry that had been brewing between us. As my feelings for him grew steadily, I remained poised and unaffected by his appeal and wit. There was also that little fact that he still had a girlfriend of three years. How do I compete with that, I thought? "Just be yourself, Deb, and whatever happens, happens" is what I told myself regularly. We both enrolled in college, even sharing a class or two, which of course meant carpooling—anything to be with him.

During this time we discovered that we wanted many of the same things and had similar goals in life, eventually becoming really good friends. He was so easy to talk to, well mannered, caring, respectful, charming, fine (what we said back in the day— "fine"), and the list goes on and on. Fuji opened doors, he pulled out chairs, and he shook hands—all the things I knew mattered to my very strict parents, particularly my dad. I was, actually still am, a daddy's girl, and it was important to me that my dad like, and eventually love, the man I wanted to spend the rest of my life with. Dad approved of Fuji immediately. Fuji and I did this song and dance for about four months. One month in I knew I loved him but refused to profess it to him. One of my best friends told me, "Deb, don't you say 'I love you first,' and even if he says it first, you should still hold out." *What?* What kind of madness is that? I'm already torn by the fact I can't say it and now I have to hold out should he say it first? My friend Michelle was only twenty-two then; what did she know about love anyway?

On October 3, 1991, I'd just finished taking a college level exam. Fuji lived minutes away from the campus we both attended, so I went to his house afterward. We were casually hanging out, watching TV, he was lying on my lap, and out of nowhere he said, "I think I'm falling in love with you."

"What?" I nervously yet excitedly all at once responded. It had been four months and finally he had uttered the words I'd been longing to hear. I also heard Michelle's voice: "Deb, don't you say it first, blah, blah, blah…" Gently I raised his chin so we were looking into each other's eyes, and I asked him, "Are you sure? Do you even know what you just said?" He said, "Yes…I love you!" Without hesitation I said, "I love you too." Sorry, Michelle. I remember it like it was yesterday.

For the next five years we grew as a couple and did everything together. Early in the relationship I discovered how selfless he was. He dropped out of community college and told me to quit working my part-time job as a sales representative at a shoe store in Aventura Mall and focus on getting my bachelor's degree. He offered to pay for any little credit card bills I had and anything I wanted. That wasn't much, but really? Who does that! The plan was that he would go back to school when I finished. Unfortunately it never happened. I would lose my mind if either of our sons did that. I often regret it because here I am not even using what I worked so hard for, not to mention the student loans I accumulated because of it. I graduated cum laude from Florida International University with a bachelor's degree in health care administration in December 1995. He certainly could have utilized his degree had he gotten one. Oh well, no use crying over spilled milk. What's done is done and everything happens for a reason. Thank goodness he found a career in banking and loved every minute of it. After years of hard work, determination, and the will to be a success story, Fuji is an independent, successful, licensed financial advisor. I am so proud of him.

The first year of the relationship, like all relationships, was fun and pretty much argument free. We were attached at the hip and inseparable. Fast-forward into our second year, the honeymoon phase was over and the bickering began. Honestly, it wasn't that bad, but we had our moments. I remember our first "big" fight. I thought it was surely over. I specifically remember telling him, "Look, if you're going to do everything I tell you to, we are not going to last. You need to grow some balls and stand up to me." *What?* I surely did, Shirley. Fuji was so sweet, yet I didn't want someone I could control. Who does? I never wanted to wear the pants in a relationship; besides, I look hotter in skirts and dresses. Well, that was the end of that. Going forward, my "controlling" him was not an issue, even though I knew that from the outside looking in, family and friends thought otherwise. I was not used to guys treating me so kindly and with respect. Most of my actions were simply reactions to what I was used to. It took some adjusting and getting used to, but I soon realized that he was different and unlike any other guy I had come in contact with. Fuji and I got married December 14, 1996, one year after I graduated from college.

Journal Entry—May 11, 2009

Well nine days ago my journal entry was quite depressing. I'm happy to say I'm not feeling quite as bad thanks to the best husband on the planet. Yesterday started really rough as well but Fuji was sweet enough to take me to lunch knowing I was bummed and as I was walking into the restaurant I happened to read a tweet from Steve Harvey that said P.U.S.H. thru which meant pray until something happens. It was just what I needed to read – lunch was great. My husband was very comforting in understanding that I'm obviously going through something. I will continue to pray and ask God for guidance and His touch on my life and my family.

Interesting Fact: Approximately 6% of American couples marry, divorce, and then re-marry each other.

CHAPTER 3

Our Lives As Newlyweds

A happy marriage is the union of two good forgivers.

~ Ruth Bell Graham

April 1997 was the official start of our new lives as husband and wife. In the midst of planning our wedding, we also had our home built in a city just three hours north of Miami—Orlando, Florida. We moved to Orlando in March, and we stayed in an extended-stay facility; one of the vilest experiences of my life. Did I mention that I'd never left my house before that time and always had the comfort of a nice, safe, and secure home with my parents? At the time of the move, we could not close on the new house until we established our jobs and had received documented proof of such—the qualifying process. This took six weeks to accomplish. During those six weeks I cried often and thought to myself, what did I just do? Why am I living in hell? At least that's what it felt like at twenty-four years old. I desperately wanted to go back home to my parents. This was not the life I envisioned. Had my parents seen where and how we were living, they might have had my marriage annulled. Even today I don't think they quite grasp my experience. The "affordable hotel alternative," or what I like to call Hotel Transylvania, was simply repulsive and desolate. At first glance it was a mere low-budget motel, one we discovered during the day. Side note: before moving anywhere or moving into anything, always do a drive by at different hours throughout the day to see what type of area you will be living in, because Lord knows the freaks come out at night.

The room was approximately 350 square feet. The bed was covered with a polyester, multicolored comforter that probably had not been washed in weeks, dare I say months. The thought sickens me. The kitchen was constructed directly in front of the bathroom—brilliant engineering, don't you think! The room was not equipped with a stove, so we bought a portable rice cooker and an electric skillet.

Chapter 3

Nothing about this unit screamed comfort or home, *nothing!* I guess when you're young and in love with the man of your dreams, you think together you can conquer anything. After evaluating and accepting our living quarters for what we thought would be only two weeks at the most, we began unloading what few belongings we had from our car and into the room.

Not long after, maybe a week later, religiously, like clockwork, we heard the neighbors fighting. They fought every single night. There were times we thought they would come crashing through the paper-thin walls. We clearly heard a young woman being punched and tossed around like a rag doll, as she screamed night after night. Rarely were her screams verbal, but more like whaling noises from being beaten. Looking back, the abuse took place more or less the same time every night—odd. We, more I, was petrified and afraid to call the police for fear of retaliation. Funny enough, we never saw them, but we definitely heard them. Consequently, we had no idea we were in one of the worst neighborhoods in Orlando. That was quickly realized, but thought we would stick it out because moving into our new home was imminent.

Edwin transferred with Washington Mutual and reported to work immediately after the move. It took me about a week to get settled into my new job as a credentialing coordinator at Principal Healthcare. That meant I hung out in that ghastly hotel room by myself for an entire week. Days passed, two weeks came and went, until finally, six painstaking weeks later, we closed on our home. Once the process was done, the real estate agent congratulated us and handed us a token gift along with the keys, and we drove back to the fortress of doom. We packed our things, returned the hotel keys, and vacated the premises within the hour. Next to saying "I do," this was the happiest day of our young lives.

The thirty-minute drive was eternal, but as we pulled into our newly developed community, ultimately approaching our driveway, a soothing sense of accomplishment came over me. As we walked toward the stained-glass double doors, Fuji inserted the key, opened the door, and then lovingly picked me up and said, "Welcome home, Mrs. Martinez." With tear-filled eyes I walked in every room, shouting, "We did it!" I even rolled around on our newly installed off-white carpet. The smell of newness was so pleasant. I did not want any remnants of Hotel Transylvania in our brand-new empty home, so the first thing we did was take all of our clothes and throw them on the grass in the backyard out in the sun. We did not realize that our clothes had absorbed the smell of cigarettes and must until we left. Now that was disgusting. I thought to myself, wow, is that what I smelled like when I went to work? My coworkers probably thought I was a chain smoker.

Here we were, newlyweds, with nothing but our cars, our clothes, and our wedding gifts. We needed everything, from a washing machine and dryer to dining room furniture, bedroom sets, kitchenware, etc. We needed it all!

Our home was the first one built in the third phase of the community. There was nothing around for at least a month, and I mean nothing, no streetlights, no people, no cars, I mean nothing! Just a newly built white house, lots of darkness, and strange critters; another environment I was not familiar with. I grew up in Miami. Not overly infested with strange critters but heavily populated with lizards and snakes, that was about it. Our community was older and established, where the neighbors barely spoke to each other. We grew up minding our own business and were very private. As you will soon see, my life in Orlando was quite the contrary.

About a month after, the rest of the homes were being built and we had neighbors, tons of them. Most of our neighbors were just like us, young and starting a family—it was perfect and so fairy tale.

Over the next few years our neighbors became our family. There were three families in particular that we bonded with right away, two to the immediate left of us and the other, five houses down the block. Two were sisters along with their husbands and kids; the other was an older retired couple. This of course was comforting to my mom, as she was so worried that we moved so far away with no family and no friends. We became so close to our neighboring families that at one point, seventeen of us were pregnant at the same time. People were afraid to visit and thought there was something in the water—rightfully so.

I've always been a planner (that stopped in my mid-thirties), so planning when to have our first child was no different. After almost two years of working and being in our home, I got pregnant in March of 1998. Four months in I thought a number of things, such as who does this, and why, and I would never do "it" again. Pregnancy was not for me. The throwing up, the nausea, and the cravings were more irritating than anything else. What I hated more than being pregnant was the response time of my husband when I said I was hungry. I was always hungry and craved just about every Jamaican dish you could think of, which, by the way, my parents came up regularly and made many of, such as oxtail, curry goat, ackee and saltfish, and stew peas. I even craved mannish water (goat head soup). Yes, you read that correctly—*goat head soup!* Anyway, back to my husband's lack of urgency when I was hungry. I always felt like when he wanted something to eat, there was always this great rush, as if the building was on fire, but when I complained about being hungry, he went into sloth mode. What the heck? Yes, this almost always lead to an argument. Side note, husbands: when your wife is pregnant, it's *always* about her and *never* about you…*always!* The sooner you accept that the easier dealing with her pregnancy becomes—happy wife, happy life.

Nine months later, after many bouts of emotional and physical ups and downs, forty pounds heavier, now a waddling 201-pound mammoth, I gave birth to our first child, Christian Edwin Martinez. I was scheduled to be induced one week prior to the original due date because the doctor knew Christian was going to be a big baby. Besides that, my back could no longer handle the pressure. My scheduled induction began at about eight o'clock one Friday morning. After thirty-one hours of labor, three epidurals, and a C-section, our son arrived on Saturday, December 12, 1998, at a whopping nine pounds and three ounces. No wonder I couldn't deliver him. I swear that child's head was the same size at birth as it is now—he finally grew into it.

After spending four days in the hospital, it was time to take our new baby home. I made Edwin take the back roads because I was afraid to get on the highway with our new baby boy. Anything over thirty-five miles per hour was too fast; even going over speed bumps and driving on cobblestone roads was too much to bear. Side note, men: now it's about your wife *and* the new baby...you, not important...not yet at least! Finally, we made it home safely. I kept Christian protected at home; he never left the house for the first month. I was very protective of Christian, like most first-time mothers would be. I had bottles of sanitizers throughout the house. I did whatever it took to keep him healthy.

When the baby was one month old, I realized how much I loved sleep. I recall sitting in the corner of Christian's room, trying to rock him to sleep at two o'clock in the morning, and all I did was cry. Looking back I'm certain I was experiencing a combination of things, including fatigue and postpartum depression. All my young friends were going through the same thing, so we had no clue how to console each other. We often used comedy to console each other. Finally, Fuji came into the room and asked me, "What's wrong?" I sobbingly responded, "All I want to do is sleep." After that, I think he had night duties and I had day duties (with both kids)…whew! That was a tremendous relief. That was also wonderful for my husband to assume that responsibility without me having to ask. This is only one of the many examples of how amazing my husband is and why I give him sex whenever he wants it. Do you know how many times I've told that story and men have looked at me as if I had three eyes and a set of horns and were bold enough to respond, "No sir, not me. That is the woman's responsibility." To that I often have said, "Yeah, OK, maybe in your house, but not mine." Raising our family was never *my* job, it was *our* job. After all, we created them together, we were going to raise them together, whatever that meant to us. As the years went on, we compromised.

After three months of being home with our new baby, it was time to go back to work. Initially Christian stayed with a neighbor. Over the course of the next five years, my baby went to seven different day-care facilities and private sitters. These were by far some of the most stressful and difficult times for me as a new mom. I vowed I would never have more children if we were not financially able to care for them at home until they were ready for school.

I know this may not be feasible for most, but it's one piece of advice I like to share with women. It makes a huge difference in the child's life. So back to work I went, and life went on as we knew it.

Journal Entry—October 9, 2009

Today was a beautiful day. First because I woke up and saw my two beautiful sons and handsome hubby. I didn't do much today but it was super. I went grocery shopping and worked at Pizza Friday at the school. Fuj surprised me and showed up to help. I love when he surprises me like that. So once finished we came home, fed the boys, and he announced that he made plans for Nadine to watch the boys and we would go on a date. I was like what? Anyhoot we got dressed, went and grabbed something to eat and went to see "Couples Retreat" – it was very good! The best part was it only cost us $40. Amazing!!! Perfect with our budget. Then we came home, walked a mile and of course made love. What a great day it was.

Interesting Fact: Marrying younger than age 25 dramatically raises the divorce risk. Also, the divorce risk is higher when the woman is much older than the man, though the reverse isn't as a strong factor.

CHAPTER 4

Surviving Our First Tragic Loss Together

Remember: the course of true love is filled with obstacles.

~ Unknown

In August of 2001 I discovered I was about eight weeks pregnant with our second child. We were excited. Coincidentally, friends and family happened to be at our home at the time of discovery, so without hesitation we shared the exciting news. Unfortunately, the excitement was short lived. One Saturday morning my husband and I made love like we did regularly. On this day things were somewhat different. I went to the bathroom and noticed I was bleeding. I was a little scared but thought nothing of it, as I know it's normal to experience spotting with pregnancies. I called over my girlfriends, all three of them, and they reassured me that I would be fine, that it was nothing to be overly concerned about, especially after speaking with the doctor. A few hours went by, the bleeding continued, and the pain intensified. I called my doctor once again, nervously explaining what I was experiencing. After asking me a series of questions, he proceeded to inform me that I may be having a miscarriage and should head to the hospital immediately.

Between the phone call and getting in the car, so much transpired. As quickly as I could, I got dressed and, barely making it out of the house, I bled profusely and started vomiting blood in the yard. Eventually I got into the car, and Fuji was able to get me to the hospital as quickly and safely as he could. He ran every toll and light he came across. It took him about fifteen minutes to get to the emergency room on the opposite side of town. Once we got there, I walked into the emergency room and told the ER nurse what was happening. She rudely responded that I needed to wait. Thank God for the angel who was sitting with her and said, "It's OK, I will wait, attend to her." I continued to bleed and the sharp, stabbing pains worsened. I clearly recall moments that I thought I was going to die. The ER staff were able to get me into a room and performed a sonogram immediately. Initially the technician was very calming and said everything would be fine— what they are trained to do. She tried to comfort me by talking me through the process. Then she said she wasn't able to detect anything, so she had to perform a vaginal ultrasound. This time she remained quiet and quickly went outside to get the doctor. Soon after, they both returned to the room with devastating news.

"Debbie, I'm terribly sorry, but you had an ectopic pregnancy and you've lost the baby. I'm going to go in through your navel and try to save your tube. If I'm unable to do so, I will need to perform another C-section and remove it that way." By this point I was in so much pain I didn't care what he did, I just didn't want to be in pain anymore. This entire ordeal began at ten o'clock in the morning, and it was now approximately eight o'clock at night. After waiting eternally for an anesthesiologist, I finally went into surgery at ten o'clock, twelve painful hours later. The next time I awoke it was nine o'clock the next morning and I was heavily sedated. The doctor came in and said the surgery was a success and I could go home in a day or two. He explained all that he did and that I would still be able to conceive, even with one tube. He left and I cried. I felt so alone and broken.

As the day went on I had visitors in and out. It was by far the worse hospital experience I've ever had. Not only did I lose my baby; the care after the surgery was simply horrible. I had the most insensitive nurses all rotating during my stay at the hospital. After waking up from surgery, one of the nurses told my friend not to assist me with anything and that I needed to get up and go take a bath. Her lack of compassion, coupled with my inability to do anything, was a terrifying mix. For three days I endured similar treatment from other nurses. I thought to myself, isn't it enough that I lost my baby? To have to deal with this level of service was too much to bear.

The moment came and it was time to leave. As my husband pushed me through the halls of the hospital in a wheelchair, I watched other moms leave with their newborns. All I left with was a bouquet of flowers. That was a tough pill to swallow.

The subsequent days were rough, physically, mentally, and emotionally. I remember the following

Tuesday morning all too well. As I lay in bed, legs elevated, watching the morning news, I witnessed the attack of September 11. At the time my sister-in-law lived only blocks away from the Twin Towers. My husband was at work when he heard the news. He spoke with her as she made her way through the second building while it was being hit. Moments later they lost contact. It was one of the longest day of our lives. Eventually we heard from her. She was understandably devastated but safe. That same week I learned that a dear friend of mine's cancer had returned. As a result of all that had occurred that week, I selflessly put my experience on the back burner and never really mourned the loss of my child. It wasn't until the week before Thanksgiving, on my way home from work, that I pulled over on the side of the road and sobbed. As I sat crying alone in my car, it dawned on me that I was no longer pregnant. To be quite honest I still get emotional talking about it, so I'm not quite sure I *ever* mourned the loss of my baby.

I honestly don't recall Edwin and me really talking about the miscarriage, in part because of all that had happened in the space of one week. Even though I know he had to have been saddened by our loss, I'm not quite sure it's affected him the way it has me. I think the way we dealt with it was to pack our bags and leave town for a few days. We spontaneously drove to Georgia to surprise my brother, who had just closed on his new home. For the next few days we basked in his celebration and downplayed our loss. My advice, should you be faced with loss or something so devastating: Never assume that your spouse is fine. Seek some sort of counseling, or, if not, at least have conversations about what happened. We all deal with loss differently.

Journal Entry—January 8, 2012

Whoa I'm on a roll writing in my journal. I promised to do better in writing in here, not only when I'm down and bummed when things are great too. Today we went to church, always feels good. Came home made a big breakfast and watched a movie with the family, then made love to the love of my life; he's so wonderful. My husband and my kids are the one thing that are a constant in my life and for that I'm so grateful.

Interesting Fact: A person's level of education influences the age at which they marry. Couples tend to marry later in states with higher numbers of college-educated adults, while the opposite is true for states with lower education levels.

CHAPTER 5

My Professional Challenges While Chasing The Dream

If you don't know what your passion is, realize that one reason for your existence on earth is to find it.

~ Oprah Winfrey

Pursuing your dream or doing what you were truly created to do can come at any age and at any time in your life. I'm living proof of that. Be open and aware of that still, small voice, the one that not even God's strongest force of nature can drown out. The one that wakes you up in the middle of the night. So often we spend our time trying to figure out what our purpose is, even talking to others about what we should do, when we've known all along through that still, small voice. Don't ignore it! "God is not just the starting point of your life; he is the *source* of it. To discover your purpose in life, you must turn to God's word, not the world's wisdom." ~ Rick Warren

By the time I was thirty-one years old, I was married with two kids, had a pretty decent career in corporate America, and was established—had a home and two fairly new cars, life seemed great. To this point I was living but not feeling fulfilled or passionate about what I did for a living. For years I would come home from work and Fuji would ask, "How was your day?" Usually the first thing I responded was, "I'm depressed." I honestly think I may have said it for about ten years. That's a long time to express such a negative phrase. Words are very powerful and, if said repeatedly long enough, they can have long-lasting effects. Sometimes I wouldn't even think about what I said. It became so natural to respond that way.

I got my bachelor's degree in health care administration in December 1995, landing my first job with Humana in Miramar, Florida, as a credentialing coordinator. I excelled quickly and was selected to represent the company to provide training to fellow employees in Louisville, Kentucky, with my area manager. It was my first professional business trip at twenty-five years old; this was awesome! I felt like an adult. I worked in my area of expertise for almost two years but soon realized I was bored and didn't love it; there had to be more to corporate America than this. I worked with Humana for a while, eventually resigning.

Fast-forward approximately two years. We were married and relocated to Orlando, where my first job in the new city was also as a credentialing coordinator, but with Principal HealthCare—boring! That too was short lived. I started to seek opportunities elsewhere and eventually worked as an office administrator with a commercial mortgage banking firm as a temp-to-perm hire. Three months later I was offered a position as a production coordinator in a field I knew nothing about, but because it was different it was now a challenge. The increase in salary was about eight thousand dollars a year, so without hesitation I said, "Absolutely, why not?" I worked fewer hours for more money and I had a set schedule. As a new mommy and wife, that was essential to me. The other great thing about this job was it provided new challenges, as the field was completely foreign. I worked alongside some of the best in the business.

Over the course of five years I worked as a production coordinator, eventually becoming the office manager. Shortly thereafter, I hit yet another glass ceiling. Again I found myself uninterested and had no desire to pursue what once seemed so exciting. Yes, I got bored quickly. Boredom is a telltale sign that you are not doing what you are supposed to be doing and it's time to move on. However, never quit until you have something else lined up. Let's be real; we have bills to pay. Meanwhile, my husband's career was flourishing and moving in the direction he wanted and had been working toward. Remember, he'd sacrificed his college education for me, and his hard work and above-average intelligence carried him far. Edwin began his banking career as a teller at Great Western and quickly accelerated to a number of positions that eventually took him to what he successfully became, an independent financial advisor with his own company, Focal Wealth Management.

Feeling trapped, I decided to explore banking. Surely I would find success in banking. Growing up, anything in banking was a highly revered position to hold. There was so much room for growth, I was able to interact with different people daily, and the opportunity to make a decent living was excellent, so the possibilities were endless. I found a position as a platform banker in 2002 with Washington Mutual, but it meant taking a severe pay cut, as it was partly commission based. Because I knew my work ethic, I thought it wouldn't be long before I got promoted, so I took the job.

Soon after I began working at the bank, I found out I was pregnant with our second child. Remember I vowed that if I could not be a stay-at-home mom until my child was at least three, I would not get pregnant again. I truthfully enjoyed this job. I worked with a great team of fellow bankers, many of whom I am still friends with. Working at Washington Mutual was rewarding most times. I was able to solve our customers' problems, whether it was simply refunding a nonsufficient charge or getting them approved for a home equity loan. Unfortunately, in January of 2003, I made the very difficult decision to resign from the bank despite holding a position I truly enjoyed. Later that month I gave birth to a beautiful, seven-pound-nine-ounce baby boy we named Zachary Alexander Martinez. He was beautiful, and not just in my opinion, but in the nurses' as well. They repeatedly said over and over again, "He is so beautiful." At one point I asked, "Are you sure it's not a girl?" How often are baby boys referred to as beautiful? So I was confused for a minute. I asked because we didn't know the sex of the baby ahead of time; we wanted it to be a surprise. Throughout the pregnancy, everyone had me convinced I was having a girl. After all, I carried differently than I did with

Christian and I gained ten pounds less. Rarely was I sick, and I did not have the crazy cravings like I did with our first. Anyway, at the time of delivery, for five brief seconds I was disappointed at the announcement that it was another boy until I saw his beautiful face and counted his precious fingers and toes. The nurses were right, he was "beautiful."

Everything from being pregnant to the delivery with Zachary was different and a less stressful experience. Because my first delivery was a C-section, the doctor suggested the second should be as well. He got no argument from me. I've often said I would love to be the poster child for C-sections; there is no pain, they are scheduled, I got my hair and nails done—it was a breeze. Delivering Zachary was a scene straight out of a soap opera.

So here I was, a stay-at-home mom with my now nine-month-old and a toddler, and what happened? A part-time position became available! At this point my mom had relocated from Miami to Orlando and lived literally eight minutes away from our home—it was perfect! It appeared as if all the pieces of the puzzle were starting to fit. My mom happily took care of Zachary, Christian was in preschool, and I went back to work. I could do it all, pursue my career, and not worry about my children, as I knew they were in good hands. The part-time position was ideal. It was from nine o'clock until two o'clock and literally ten minutes from home. Rarely does it get any better than that.

Don't hold your breath, though. I had the manager from hell! He was adamant about making my life miserable. His newly appointed position to my branch location was disruptive on every level. We were doing well financially, so there was no need to tolerate the misery he caused daily. My husband supported me and said if I did not want to work but instead stay home permanently with our kids, I could, and so I quit. I decided to go home and be a full-time stay-at-home mom to my now one-year-old child. Now this, I loved. I did everything with him. He was truly the perfect baby. He made me consider having more. Notice I said "me" and not "us." My hubby wanted no part of it. He had known he didn't want any more kids since I became pregnant with Zachary. He thought two were enough. He didn't want to be outnumbered, or was it my hormonal ups and downs that made him come to that conclusion? I might never know.

Fast-forward to 2006. For whatever reason, both my husband and my cousin Janice started this constant harassment about me getting back into modeling. They did this persistently for about two years and I boldly said, *"No!"* They thought my smile, personality, and sense of humor should be seen. Yes, I'd matured and come a long way from that self-conscious, skinny nineteen-year-old. However, I was then a size 12/14 and was feeling very insecure about my body. That's a long way from the size 0/2 I'd been used to most of my life. (Can I please find a happy medium?) My cousin proceeded to tell me that plus-size models start at a size 8 and there's tons of work for them. I laughed uncontrollably and still said *no*. I questioned her a little only because she said she had a friend who was a plus-size model and was doing well in New York. Still, I was not 100 percent convinced, but I admit I gave it a little thought.

Pause and rewind. It's important you understand where this was all coming from. I started modeling in South Florida when I was thirteen years old with basic modeling courses. I pursued it until I was about twenty-two. It was something I'd always wanted to do. At five feet ten inches tall, 119 pounds, I was meant to be a model—at least so I thought. For years, without ever having an agent, I did odd jobs—none of which I ever got paid for. I entered contests and won, appeared in music videos, was an extra in a few movies, and still nothing ever came of it. Finally I took it upon myself to hire a photographer. I had some head shots done and walked into the two biggest and best-known modeling agencies on South Beach. In short, the first one said, "I'm sorry but we are looking for blondes with bigger boobs." The other said, "You should have come when you were fourteen or fifteen, and you are too heavy." Those words permeated every ounce of my body. I remember it like it was yesterday. Did I mention that I was five feet ten inches tall and weighed in at a whopping 119 pounds? I mean seriously, I would turn sideways and disappear! I was the platform for skinny-girl jokes.

I took my black-and-white head shots, tears at the cusp of streaming down my face, and nervously walked out of the agency. I took extra-long strides to my car on that beautiful, sunny, South Florida day and sat in the car and balled my eyes out. I cried for the duration of the ride home, which was about forty minutes. It was a heartbreaking day for me. At the age of twenty-two, how many people can honestly say they are comfortable in their skin, they have great self-esteem, are extremely confident, and feel beautiful and attractive? Not me! I was so awkward. Back then full lips and big, crazy hair were not in. I remember outlining my lips on the inside to make them look less full. Now I boldly show my lips! We'll talk about my confidence later.

It was during this forty-minute ride home that I made the decision that I would finish college, get married, and move away, basically suppressing and giving up on my dream. So said, so done. Mentally I dug a hole and buried my greatest desires. Fuji and I were dating at the time and he supported anything I wanted to do.

Back to my husband's and cousin's incessant harassment about me pursuing modeling. I'd given it some thought, and four months had passed from that last conversation with my cousin about becoming a plus-size model. Her younger sister, my baby cousin Nadine, informed me about a model search coming to Orlando, for all ages, I believe. She said, "Cuz, I think you should enter." Sigh. OK, here we go again. I hired a photographer, took some shots, and entered this ridiculous model search—which I later found out was a big hoax. Even though it was a hoax, I was supposedly "one of the nine hundred who were chosen out of the ten thousand in the entire state" who entered. It was just the boost I needed. Later that year, around August of 2007, I enrolled in a twelve-week acting class at a local modeling and acting school, The Maile School. I thought I would take acting courses and use them as a back door to pursue modeling. I was never interested in acting because I was fearful of memorizing long, tedious scripts. I thought it would also give me time to lose some of my baby weight. Let's face it, in this business you have to look good at all times, so in addition to classes, I also hired a professional fitness trainer to help me get back into shape. I completed the course and something unexpected happened: I fell in love with acting! Two weeks after completing the course, I booked two short student films, and the rest is history. I've been working ever since and have made quite a name for myself here in Central Florida.

I worked the first year strictly on referrals from the modeling school and without an agent. Better than that, I got paid for the small parts I did book. One year in and I had enough experience to produce a resume. Finally, I signed with my very first agency, DK Model and Talent. Even though they are no longer in business, I will always be grateful because they took a chance on a no-name, thirty-five-year-old mother of two. A few years in and I've done it all: modeling, acting, hosting, voice-overs, industrials, emceeing, being a guest speaker, being an instructor, even doing stunts—who knew! Finally, I was living the very dream I'd mentally buried years ago.

Why bury the dream? Figure out ways to make it work! It might mean making sacrifices, and great big ones, but in the end you'll be glad you took the risk and made those sacrifices. I made a huge sacrifice to pursue my dream job by not going back to corporate

America and receiving a guaranteed five-figure income—that's a ginormous sacrifice! You don't know what happy is (outside of your family, etc.—strictly referring to your career here) until you are truly doing what you love. It's the best feeling in the world when I'm working doing what I enjoy. I feel guilty calling it work—even guiltier because I get paid to do it!

Journal Entry—April 16, 2012

I'm so disappointed in myself. We've been here eleven days and this is only my second entry. What I will say is it has been fun but also a little emotional. I've never left my family for this long but thanks to my loving husband he brought the boys and drove 6 hours to spend the weekend with me. Even though it was super short I'm still grateful they came, not to mention our love making…it was phenomenal. I love this man so much. He makes my heart shiver and smile all at once. Anyway this will be my last week in Atlanta for now. I have a shoot in Orlando on 4/24/12 but I will be back soon. This new market hasn't seen the last of D. Foxx yet, it's only the beginning.

Interesting Fact: Experts note that if a spouse has gained more than 20% of his or her body weight, divorce is more likely.

CHAPTER 6

Losing Everything...Just About!

Loving can cost a lot, but not loving can cost a lot more.

~ M. Shain

Edwin was thriving and doing substantially well, making six figures as a financial advisor. The real estate market was prosperous and it seemed as though everyone was benefiting from it—bankers, real estate agents, investors, homeowners...everyone! Homes were increasing in value by ten percent to thirty percent, depending upon the year. It was incredible. Florida became the hot spot. Northerners were selling their homes for hundreds of thousands of dollars and then purchasing something here, two, maybe even three times the size, with that money. They were moving here by the droves.

Because the real estate market was doing so well, we thought it would be wise to invest in the market and plan for our children's future. In the summer of 2005, we decided to research buying rental properties in different markets. We'd owned rental properties before, so why not? After months of research, we came across a small town in Georgia known as Albany. It was a quiet, quaint little town where everyone knew everyone. It was clearly a tight-knit community. We took several weekend trips there, eventually meeting the Barfields. The Barfields were well-known in Albany and owned lots of real estate there. We met with them on numerous occasions, visiting their million-dollar estate on massive acres of land and being comfortably chauffeured around in their luxury 7-series BMW. They were kind and treated us with true Southern hospitality. We respected and admired them, as they were consummate professionals in the business. Mr. Barfield took a particular liking to us and served somewhat as a mentor. I think he liked us because he appreciated our ambitious undertakings as a young couple.

The Barfields had a small parcel of land on which they planned to build eight quadruplexes (one building with four individual units). They were all for sale and at a reasonable price. After careful consideration and having our finances reviewed, we thought this would be a great way to prepare for Christian's and Zachary's college funds and our future. We'd planned on naming it Martinez Row—talk about big dreams and visions. We began the process and took a second loan out on our home. We then purchased four of those quads, which meant we were now the proud owners of sixteen rental units.

This wasn't enough! We came across a townhouse, literally two miles away from our primary residence, and we purchased it at preconstruction price, a bargain. We made money on it prior to completion. We were on a roll and an indescribable high. We felt so accomplished. It was official: by mid-2006 we were landlords/investors of seventeen rental units! Life was great! On paper we were millionaires. We had a healthy 401(k), we owned vacant land, we had rental properties, *we* were beyond living the American dream.

In addition to becoming landlords, we did lots and lots of traveling. For approximately four consecutive years, we took anywhere from four to six trips per year, some with the kids and some without. We spent several summers touring the West Coast of the United States. We spent days at a luxury hotel, the Fairmont Olympic Hotel, in Seattle, Washington, near the famous Pike Place Market (a must visit, by the way, if you've never been). We did several sightseeing adventures there, such as Chateau Ste. Michelle and the well-known Space Needle. We visited Santa Fe, New Mexico. There we experienced fly fishing in twenty-degree weather, attended parties hosted by millionaires in their fifteen-thousand-square-foot adobe homes, had dinners with chief financial officers and other affluent businesspeople. San Diego, Palm Springs, Temecula, Los Angeles, Santa Barbara, Simi Valley, all cities in California, were not off limits either. The adventures were never ending. Many of these trips were courtesy of Edwin's job and his performance as a financial advisor. All have been meticulously documented via an old hobby—scrapbooking.

And then came the debacle. For approximately three years we maintained all seventeen units with humility, pride, and lots of hard work. We did the best we could, and for a while things were going great—*until* the collapse of the real estate market.

We went from 95 percent occupancy to 50 percent occupancy, which meant we were paying for those mortgages out of our pockets. Our tenants lost their jobs, forcing them to relocate or move in with other family members. Some were even evicted for nonpayment. Even though Edwin's income was substantial, managing the properties was short lived and too much to handle. We held on as long as we could, hoping things would change, but sadly they never did.

Late in 2008 Edwin suggested multiple times that we should file bankruptcy, but without hesitation I responded, "Not a chance. We are not doing that. This too shall pass and it will work out. Have faith!" Was I in denial? Absolutely! Was I consumed by thoughts of the embarrassment and shame that the stigma of bankruptcy would cause? Most definitely!

By the spring of 2009 it was by far one of the toughest pills to swallow, but we were drowning, and bankruptcy became the *only* option. Bill collectors called our house relentlessly. Eventually we just took the phone of the hook…for weeks, even months at a time. I remember weeping for days. I often say that of the 365 days in 2009, I might have cried 350 of those days. Here we were trying to establish something to better ourselves, our lives, and prepare for the future, and instead it all came tumbling down like a Slinky making its way down a steep set of stairs.

We sought the help of an attorney and got a consultation scheduled immediately. It's funny how clearly I remember some of these days—I wish I could forget. Writing this book has forced me to recollect details that still hurt to my core. I remember sitting in the attorney's office desperately fighting the tears as she explained our options. As she went through the list of all of our assets, she simply said, "With the exception of the home in which you are currently residing in, I suggest you give it all up." This included the brand new Mazda CX-9 Edwin bought for me on *his* birthday. Another painful memory was sitting at home one day, the kids were in school, and suddenly the doorbell rang. I opened the door and the young lady asked if I was Debbie Martinez, to which I replied yes. The individual handed me papers and told me we were being served. I opened the envelope, and in brief it said our home was being foreclosed. After reading it I sat on my sofa, clutched a cushion, and bawled my eyes out. Thoughts about being homeless, with nowhere to go, engulfed my mind.

Chapter 6

Fuji came home shortly and I told him what had happened. As usual he was very nonchalant (a quality often admired by most, including me—nothing phased this man), but, looking back, this is how he dealt with the stresses of life. Without him knowing, I visited the lawyer's office the next day, obviously unnerved by the whole thing. I waited for a while and finally someone asked how she could help. There was a slight language barrier with the individuals who worked in the front office, which was also very frustrating. Anyway, after telling them about receiving the papers, I asked if someone could briefly explain what it truly meant. To that they responded, "Ma'am it's going to cost you $50 for someone to tell you what the papers mean." On cue I broke down wailing, as streams of tears rolled down my face and I became a blubbering mess. I pled, "Can someone please help me? I don't understand what these papers mean and all I want to know is, am I being kicked out of my house and, if so, how much time do I have to get out?"

I guess they felt sorry for me, because they escorted me to an office and in minutes my questions were answered and I was briefly consoled, and, no, we did not get kicked out of our home. I could go on and on about the many stories that took place before, during, and after the bankruptcy, but I won't. Even though I'm over the stigma of being embarrassed about filing bankruptcy, it's still a bit much to bare recall all that we lost.

By the summer of 2009 all the paperwork had been done, so we went to court and explained our circumstances to the judge. Even though we had not done anything wrong, I was so annoyingly nervous that my legs bounced uncontrollably, I picked at my nails, I had visions of us going to jail—it was insane! Another day I wish I could forget. The judge proceeded to ask us a line of questions in an intense and intimidating manner. Fortunately for me, Edwin was there, because I heard nothing. All I saw were the judge's lips moving, but nothing audible came out. Even though I knew our situation was common, people filing bankruptcy left and right, not once did I find comfort in that. Instead, I felt ashamed, embarrassed, and disappointed. I felt like I'd let my family down. Edwin felt all of these emotions and then some as the man of our household. Going to court was the last step of the process. In October we received our discharge papers. The burden was lifted and now it was time to start over and rebuild.

Chapter 6

The icing on the cake was receiving a phone call mid-November from a repossession representative/detective. He informed me that he needed to come and get the SUV and that the repossession process was in place. He said, "Mrs. Martinez, I'm an officer of the law. Please do not destroy the vehicle in any way. I know this may be heartbreaking, and to prevent any further embarrassment you can leave the vehicle in a public parking lot nearby and we will come and get it. This will avoid having it towed from your home." Officer of the law? What? Is this nightmare and the legion of embarrassments ever going to end? I felt like a criminal. I said, "Absolutely, no problem," and we agreed on a location. A few days before our son's birthday and Christmas, I drove the car to a public parking lot with Fuji following closely behind. I got out, left the keys in the SUV, locked the door as I was instructed to do, looked at it, and walked away. I sat in the car with Fuji and again I wept. I didn't cry because I was losing a material possession; I cried because of *how* we lost it, and it was the last thing to go.

Despite the series of events, Fuji and I somehow grew closer instead of growing apart, which I found truly amazing. Did you know that financial hardship is one of the top five reasons couples get divorced? Some even commit suicide. Yes, we had our moments of self-inflicted battles and blame, which led to arguments, but we never spoke of or even considered getting a divorce. The days that I spent crying and depressed about our situation, Fuji still found it in himself to be encouraging and regularly reassured me that we were going to be fine and that we would bounce back. Rarely did he break down, but he did, as he thought he had failed me, us, our family. That was very difficult to witness. Despite his feeling like a failure, he always had a great story or an analogy that made his plea believable. Even today I am truly amazed we made it through. I would never wish this on my worst enemy.

Now here we are, years later, feeling more hopeful than ever, knowing and believing that we have only just begun and that the bankruptcy was just a bump in the road that we needed to go over. Of course, as you're going through the storm it's difficult to envision the light at the end of the tunnel or the rainbow that awaits you, but, believe it or not, it's an experience I now don't regret. Not to mention, it was loaded with valuable lessons. Everything happens for a reason, even this! All it has done is prepare us for what's to come "and truly taught us to be better managers of our finances.

In January of 2009 we went to church like we do most Sundays, and the sermon was about tithing. It was a three-part sermon entitled "The Blessed Life," by Robert Morris. The series talked about the importance of tithing. In the past we believed in tithing, but it was never a priority. Paying those mortgages was always a priority, and of course the Chases, MasterCards, and American Expresses of the world. I specifically remember Edwin getting paid, on numerous accounts, five figure commission checks, but at the time our priority was distorted and tithing was rarely done. Ever since that sermon, having read *"The Blessed Life"* from cover to cover *twice,* our tithe check is the *first* check we write each pay period without hesitation. This means we are putting God first and trusting He will make the necessary provisions for us with what is left. It's not the other way around: pay all your bills first and whatever is left, *then* you tithe—that is incorrect! It's trusting, believing, and having faith in knowing that He will provide. The Bible states: *Bring all the tithes into the storehouse so there will be enough food in my temple. If you do, says the Lord of Heaven's armies, "I will open the windows of heaven for you. I will pour out a blessing so great you won't have enough room*

to take it in! Try it! Put me to the test!" (Malachi 3:10).
This book has brought me such great comfort. The
stories and analogies are relatable, not to mention
inspiring. I encourage you to do two things: first, read
it, and second, begin tithing. It will change your life,
priorities, and perspective.

Journal Entry—June 22, 2008

*Ok so on June 13ᵗʰ I had the meltdown of all
meltdowns. After writing out the bills with Fuji
on Saturday I was a hot mess. In short, the rental
properties are really starting to take a toll on us
financially, without them we would be great, just
fine! I guess I must consider it some sort of lesson
learned. I felt as if a horse had kicked me right in
the chest when Fuj decided we were going to file
bankruptcy. For the past seven years we worked so
hard to achieve good credit, 720+ and now it was
all about to be sent to hell. Luckily that day I had to
work with HSN. It took my mind of things at least
for the moment. I don't recall feeling so crappy for
so long and it sucks!*

Interesting Fact: Compared to singles, married people
accumulate about four times more savings and assets. Those
who divorced had assets 77% lower than singles.

CHAPTER 7

What Drives Me To Succeed

Our greatest weakness lies in giving up. The most certain way to succeed is always to try just one more time.

~ Thomas A. Edison

There are a number of people and factors that drive me to succeed. I'm so fixated on being successful at my craft that the constant needling of various work-related thoughts day in and day out is difficult to overlook. At times these thoughts can be consuming, but they serve as a chronic reminder that I'm living my purpose. The level of determination burns so deep it's impossible to ignore.

Most importantly, I'm driven by the one I serve, the Almighty, the Alpha and Omega, my sole Creator, the one and only, my Father in heaven. I'm very spiritual, not religious, and believe that without Him there is no me; that is first and foremost. It's through my Creator that I'm blessed with the talents I have and the gifts I've been given. There's nothing perfect about my life, but some aspects come pretty close. I believe this is so because I meditate regularly, I pray often, and being grateful is not an option but mandatory. These are my rituals first thing in the morning and the last thing before going to sleep most days. My days are not promised to me, and through my meditating and praying, I find comfort in whatever lies ahead.

Secondly, my children and my husband play a pivotal role in my success. Both of my children are pretty positive, supportive, and encouraging for their very young age. They are like this because as parents we constantly urge them to do their best and reassure them that they can do and be anything they set their minds to be. My eldest read *The Secret to Teen Power*, by Paul Harrington, at the age of ten; he was in the fifth grade. He is by far the most positive and encouraging teenager I know. He, like me, simply believes. If ever I say something like "I hope I book that job," he'll in turn say, "*When* you book that job, Mommy…" Even if I don't book the job, he'll still have something hopeful and uplifting to say. My youngest has read it as well, but the concepts have not quite kicked in yet; however, there's still time. He shows me his love and support in other ways and is very affectionate, especially toward me. I've often said that had I had their attitudes at such a young age, who knows what I may have done or become? Otherwise, granted, I have no regrets.

Then there's my husband, the ultimate advocate and supporter of my career. He by far is my biggest cheerleader. No one supersedes his role and support in my life. I remember my first year of working as a model and an actress. The entire year I thought I was too old for it and I would never get work. The whole year Fuji repetitively chanted, "There is work for everybody. Watch the commercials and you will see," and you know what, he was right. There's no one "type" of person in commercials, films, episodics, etc. There are all types of people working in this business. It took me the entire year to *believe* and acknowledge what he was saying until eventually I got it. Now I believe. Follow my work and you'll notice lots of it ends with #ibelieve.

Over the years I've steadily lost weight and am currently in the best physical shape of my life. I'm the healthiest I've ever been; my cholesterol is the lowest I've known it to be. This is a big deal to me, as members of my family have died and suffered from heart disease and other ailments that involve the heart. One exercise that has contributed to my now-healthier lifestyle is the walks I have with Fuji every night after tucking the boys in. We walk two, sometimes three miles around our neighborhood. The initial thought behind this was that it's a great cardio exercise and the dog needed to be walked. We suddenly noticed that the walks were no longer about physical activity. Instead, they became a form of therapy for both of us, probably more for me than him. We've had some amazing conversations during these walks. We've talked about our dreams, our workdays, plans for the weekends, etc. What I find most rewarding is the amount of encouragement that is given and received during these walks. During the walks there are no cell phones, television, or other people to interrupt; it is just Fuji, me, our dog, Cyrus, and the heavens that grace us with its presence most nights. Fuji encourages me on a daily basis, but when it's done during our nightly routine, it is different. I absorb it differently, I hear him loud

and clear, and it registers; there are no distractions.
Time and time again he will say things such as:

∽ "I'm so proud of you, my love."

∽ "You are such an intelligent person."

∽ "I'm amazed by your beauty."

∽ "I know you are going to be successful."

∽ "I believe in you."

∽ "You are far more talented than you realize."

∽ "You are so special."

∽ "You are so disciplined."

∽ "You're so beautiful when you are asleep."

Really, I could go on and on, but you get the picture.
Words are so incredibly powerful, and, if used in the
right manner, delivered with the right tone, they could
really change someone's life for the better. I know that
my husband's words have helped mold me into the

woman I've become today, and for that I will always be grateful. I thank God that my husband was steadfast in reciting words of reassurance and inspiration into my spirit on a regular and daily basis, even when I didn't buy into or believe what he was saying. It's almost as if he knew one day it would simply click.

Lastly, but most certainly not least, my parents, three brothers, and a host of family and friends also believe in me wholeheartedly. Sometimes it can be embarrassing going out with my parents, because that's how they like to introduce me: "Have you met my daughter, Debbie? She's on TV." With gritted teeth, forced smile, and raised eyebrows, I politely shake people's hands and quickly change the topic. For years, I wondered if I was a disappointment to my parents, especially my dad. He had such high hopes for me and wanted to see me become this top executive for high-end hotels since I once dreamt of becoming a hotelier. All through high school that was my plan *until* I worked at a luxury hotel in Miami Beach and quickly realized I hated it. I remember telling him I was changing my field of study while attending FIU, and the look of disappointment on his face was unforgettable. He wasn't sure how to respond or react. My dad always has something to say, but it was quite the contrary on that day. My brothers, on the other hand, are very low key about what I do. We are a pretty tight-knit family, and when it comes to supporting each other, we have each other's backs. My choice in career is no different in their eyes. It's what I do and it makes me happy, and that's all that matters to them. All they know is their sister is on billboards, TV, in films, and to them that means she's a star.

I cannot stress it enough that in order for you to be successful, you *must* surround yourself with people who believe in you and will support you. You are going to need them, especially on the days that you are attacked by self-doubt, fear, haters, and let's not forget the ever-busy devil. Without my family and friends, and their unwavering support, I would have *never* made it.

Each job that I've been blessed with drives me to work harder to accomplish the next set of goals. Every year I set the bar higher than the preceding year. Sometimes I may accomplish the goal, sometimes I don't, but you've heard the saying "it's better to set your goal high and miss than to aim low and make it." A great example of this took place in 2009. I had been in the business less than two years and one of my goals were to book a SAG (Screen Actors Guild) project of any type. Believe it or not, some of the naysayers in the business thought that was impossible for me because I was so new to the industry. SAG is an American union that represents hundreds of thousands of film and television principal performers worldwide. Recently it merged with the American Federation of Television and Radio Artists, so it's now referred to as SAG/AFTRA. Anyway, while attending a workshop in Miami, on my way home I received fabulous news from my then agent Robin of DK Model and Talent that I'd booked my first SAG regional commercial with Publix Supermarkets. I remember asking her over and over if she was certain it was me, and to reverify that they had not made a mistake and that she in fact read the name correctly. She assuredly said, "Deb, it was you, and you did it, congratulations!"

Receiving that news on a three-hour ride back home was great but not so great. It was great in the sense that I was completely distracted, making the journey seem more like an infamous roller-coaster ride. Not so great because I wept the entire three hours; that could have been dangerous for obvious reasons. I'd done what most hadn't done in their more seasoned careers. Booking this job now meant I was SAG/AFTRA eligible and could join the union if I so desired. Having met that goal, I raised the bar even higher and was driven to complete other

milestones. Since that project, I've had so many
other amazing opportunities, such as hosting an
online Christian talk show called *Let's Chat.* The
format was similar to that of *The View.* There were
four hosts of different backgrounds and ethnicities,
and we talked about any- and everything from a
Christian perspective. Having filmed some thirty-
six episodes as the lead host has led to many other
amazing opportunities, both directly and indirectly.
Because of this opportunity I've also picked up a lot
of behind-the-scenes, on-the-job training, for which
I will always be appreciative and is truly priceless.

Another element that drives me is the need to
achieve financial freedom. Let me preface this by
saying in no way do I pursue modeling and acting
for the wealth. Anyone that does, you are in for a
rude awakening. I do it simply because I love it!
However, I'm more than an actress and a model.
Pursuing modeling and acting has given me the
platform to do other things, and other opportunities
have presented themselves because of the two. They
are all still within the realm of the business, such
as becoming an author, a motivational speaker,
an instructor, and a talk-show host. Over the years
I've worked meticulously on building the brand of
Debra Foxx. One day it will be an empire, possibly

including a fragrance, clothing line—the possibilities are endless. I'm quite the overachiever and am open to doing anything as long as it brings me joy and satisfaction. Why? Because I believe!

I'm determined to be financially free because I want to help my family and others as well. First on the list: my parents. My parents have sacrificed so much for my siblings and me. They've been there for me spiritually, financially, emotionally, on numerous accounts. Soon I will be in the position to assume all of their financial responsibilities, allowing them more flexibility and the freedom to travel and visit faraway family members. My parents have never asked for anything in return during the good and the bad times, and for that I will eternally be indebted to them. I could never repay my parents for all they have done.

With financial freedom I'll be able to help some of my favorite charities and organizations, all of which are to benefit, aid, and assist women and children. I've had numerous girlfriends diagnosed with breast cancer over the years and have since started organizations to help local patients. I would like nothing more than to be able to contribute a generous amount of my earnings to keep those organizations going; to be involved one on one. Things that we take for granted, such as mobility and getting around daily, are things cancer patients struggle with. I'm not above taking them to their appointments, cutting their lawn, or cleaning their homes if that is what they need. If there's one thing I've learned it is that I'm not here for myself, but I'm here to serve others.

Most recently I've become a part of HOPE Now International, a nonprofit organization that provides goods and services to underprivileged families. Each year HOPE Now gives away some ten-thousand-plus backpacks stuffed with school supplies to children in need. The team of six is responsible for orchestrating the biggest backpack giveaway on the East Coast since 2008. For now I am able to donate my time, but with financial freedom I could do so much more.

Finally, I'm driven by my desire to succeed because of my love for traveling. I love discovering, learning, and exploring new cities, towns, and countries. I've never quite understood someone saying he or she has never left the state of Florida and doesn't have any interest in doing so. Traveling exposes you to wonderful and new experiences. Through traveling you could potentially discover your purpose. Traveling sparks creativity. Traveling rejuvenates, relaxes, and eases pressure and tension. The benefits of traveling are immeasurable.

My determination to flourish is undeniable. Yet I know the only way to achieve it is through continued faith and prayer, supportive family and friends, and, lastly, hard work and the ability to hustle. All of which I've done and will continue to do. Thus far it's proven that it works. My stars are aligning and soon my wildest dreams and all that I yearn will come to fruition.

Journal Entry—May 17ᵗʰ, 2011

Well I'm grateful to see the light of another day. Really and truly grateful for the relationship I have with my husband. He loves me unconditionally. I may be struggling in all areas of my life and also engaging in a series of doubtfulness but not where my husband is concerned. This past Sunday we made love with such passion. Here I am two days later still thinking about it and reminisce of his smell and touch on my body. Oh, how he loves me so. Somewhere or someone in my life blessed and prayed over my marriage (probably my mom) and I am so grateful. Thank you Lord. On another note, I'm on hold for yet another job – always the bridesmaid never the bride; my theme for 2011. Everyone seems to think something huge is in store for me. Whatever it is I welcome it with open arms. I just hope it's soon. Thank you God!

Interesting Fact: Married people are twice as likely to go to church as unmarried people.

CHAPTER 8

How We've Kept It Hot And Steamy

Remember marriage is not a contest, never keep a score. God has put the two of you together on the same team to win.

~ Zelmyra and Herbert Fisher

Keeping our relationship alive and fresh has not been difficult. I really don't understand why marriages don't work. It's not hard, but, like everything else, it does require work. It doesn't just happen, but that doesn't make it difficult.

There are a few things we have done over the years, both big and small, that have made our marriage what it is today. In no particular order, let me start off with what Fuji did for my fortieth birthday. My fortieth birthday is something we had discussed on numerous occasions, but nothing prepared me for what he did. Turning forty is supposed to be a significant time of a woman's life, a major milestone. Let me start by saying I'm not a fan of aging (I know, who is?) and he knew that all too well. I remember hating twenty-nine because thirty was around the corner. The same held true for thirty-nine; forty was knocking at the door. What I loved about turning forty, however, was how comfortable I was in my own skin. I couldn't have cared less about what people said or thought, and I loved who I was becoming as a woman.

On with the story. For one year Fuji planned the most memorable trip of my life. May I add, we've done plenty of traveling and vacationing over the past two decades, but none quite like this.

For my fortieth birthday my darling husband planned a five-day getaway to the grandiose property of Fiesta Americana Grand in lovely Cabo San Lucas, Mexico. I literally did not know where we were going until just a week or two prior, and the only reason was because I wanted to pack accordingly. I remember the morning of our trip as if it were yesterday. After traveling most of the day with one connecting flight, finally we landed in Mexico and were ready and waiting for all that was in store. After checking in at the hotel, we were upgraded to a master suite suitable for a large family, complete with a full kitchen, living room, a massive bedroom, Jacuzzi, a balcony overlooking the Pacific Ocean and hundreds of bougainvillea bushes, a beautiful, thorny bush with varicolored petals that is very common in warmer climates. Our view was simply breathtaking. We quickly dropped off our luggage and began touring the property. My vocabulary was limited to "oh my gosh" and "wow" because it was so strikingly gorgeous. The resort had five heated swimming pools and a private beach protected by its own reef. The Somma Wine Spa, a world-class golf course, was located only minutes away from the marina. Our first night we had dinner by the fire pit on the beach. I had a succulent lobster tail and Fuji had coconut curried jackfish over a mango sauce accompanied by sweet plantains—as I recall it, my mouth waters. Another memorable moment was on my actual birthday, February 14, 2012. On this morning we were both awake pretty early but did not know it, and my thinking was, we've already been here four days and I would love to see the sun rise—until that time I'd never actually watched the sun rise. So I asked Fuji if he would like to go and watch the sun rise, and without hesitation he said, "Yes, but we must hurry, it's going to happen soon." As quickly as possible we changed our clothes, washed our faces, brushed our teeth, and made our way to the opposite end of the hotel with our camera in tow. It seemed like it took forever. Luckily one of the workers had his golf cart and took us as close as he could; otherwise we might have missed it. As we turned on the camera and adjusted the settings awaiting this beautiful moment, it rose. It was as if the sun waited for me to position myself to see its striking face rise above the still waters. As it rose I cried. Words cannot express the immense feeling of gratitude, warmth, and love I felt at that very moment. I wanted to sit and watch it creep across the sky and bask in God's magical creation. Shortly after, we made our way back to the room, and of course we encountered more miraculous sightings on the walk back.

Other memorable moments were the detailed spa experience, having whales swim by our boat just a hundred feet away, having a sea lion jump on the back of our boat, being catered to on my birthday in a cabana that typically accommodates eight, and finally dinner at the Italian restaurant on my birthday night. From start to finish everything about this week was sheer perfection, and he planned it all on his own. For the next several weeks he had his way with me (wink, wink). Actually, he's still having his way!

As a family we'd often take road trips. We started this custom when our eldest was three years old. As insane as this may sound, every spring break we'd pack the car and simply head northeast. The planner that I used to be made this very difficult for me, at first, but Fuji was always about being spontaneous. After the first year I no longer needed convincing, as the trip was a huge success. Early on, my kids developed a love for historical sights, so on every road trip we sought out those places of interest. From visiting George Washington's home in Mount Vernon, Virginia, to seeing the lifestyle of the Amish in Lancaster, Pennsylvania, and even Monticello, home of President Thomas Jefferson, we couldn't get enough of our country's history. Over the years we've taken about seven or eight ten-day road trips, conquering most of the states on the East Coast and creating long-lasting memories. Do you know what kind of bonding experience is created on a ten-day road trip? Irreplaceable and priceless memories! Not to mention the invaluable history lessons for our kids. Because of these trips they have done well in their history and social studies classes.

Years ago, before getting married, Fuji and I got baptized together in a small church in Sunrise, Florida. We tried to live a Christian lifestyle, but it was trying and difficult at times. Let's be honest: it still is. Once we got married and moved, it took some time to find a new church home, and even when we did, we backslid. Fast-forward to 2009: facing our financial hardship, we found ourselves back in the church—no coincidence there. The Lord works in mysterious ways. We've since recommitted and reaffirmed our lives to God. Our kids were baptized as well. Often we read our Bibles together, we fast together, and we pray together most nights before going to bed. I have to believe that God has played an instrumental role in our lives. I often say someone prayed hard over my relationship as part of why it's so successful—I think it was my mom. She loves him to death.

Finally, without getting too detailed and specific, ever heard the term "spooning"? Basically while you are in bed the man holds you closely from behind, creating a spooning effect, so your butt is in his penis area, and you can be clothed or not. This is how we go to bed and how we wake up. Even though we have a king-sized bed, I think it's a waste of space, because the way we sleep, we are only using a mere fraction of the bed. Hmmm, that's a thought—we should trade it in for a twin, that's all we need. We cannot sleep without touching each other. If we are not spooning, then our feet are intertwined, his hand is in my hair, something must be touching. With that said, we have an amazing sex life. Our sex life is so incredibly juicy, I'm often amazed that we *still* enjoy each other with such great passion and zest. It's a wonderful thing!

A lot of what I mentioned above was grand and could be considered costly, but those are not the only things we do to keep it fresh. Here are some other things you could do to keep your relationship new:

∾ Throughout this book I've probably thrown technology by the wayside when it comes to your relationship, but here is one simple and easy way it could be used for good. Throughout the day you can send your spouse a loving and spontaneous text message. They can even be scheduled (don't do this often).

∾ Make time for date night. This can be as big or as small as you want it. For example, visit a wine bar and treat yourselves to a wine tasting with cheese. This is really affordable and makes for great conversation. Just think about all that you could learn together about wines.

∾ Send each other love notes. Secretly place them in purses, workbags, lunch bags, even on their pillows as they are getting out of the shower and ready for bed.

∾ Praise your soul mate and show appreciation regularly. Instead of focusing on what he or she doesn't do, focus on the positive. This is a great way to keep things fresh.

∾ Make love often! Notice I said "make love," not "have sex." Intimacy makes sex more pleasurable, gratifying, and authentic. Intimacy in a relationship is typically placed on the back burner behind kids, school, career, housework. It's time to make it a high priority and schedule lovemaking sessions.

Not in the mood? Get in the mood by playing some of your favorite songs, lighting your favorite scented candles, using perfumes or body oils. Do whatever it takes to get in the mood. Yes, it's work, but your relationship is worth it, and it needs it. Like everything else, if not fed, this too will wither away and die!

These are just some of the things we do to keep it exciting. Ever heard of or read the book *The 5 Love Languages,* by Gary Chapman? Elisabeth Hasselbeck, former cohost of *The View,* said, "It changed my marriage." My primary love language is *physical touch.* Here's what was stated about *physical touch:*

Physical touch: This language isn't all about the bedroom. A person whose primary language is physical touch is, not surprisingly, very touchy. Hugs, pats, on the back, holding hands, and thoughtful touches on the arm, shoulder, or face—they can all be ways to show excitement, concern, care, and love. Physical presence and accessibility are crucial, while neglect or abuse can be unforgivable and destructive. Physical touch fosters a sense of security and belonging in any relationship.

Words of affirmation and *quality time* were a close second. I felt the test was pretty accurate.

Journal Entry—January 4, 2012

I could kick myself for waiting so long to write in my journal. Well 2011 is long gone so what choice do I have but to embrace and welcome 2012 and all that it has in store for me. As usual my husband is the best. We've been up under each other every day since 12/14/2011 for the holidays and it's been wonderful. How did I get so lucky to be blessed with such a wonderful soulmate? This man is 99% perfect. I feel so safe and secure with him. Thanks you God. Christmas was very light but good. My parents celebrated their 40th wedding anniversary and we threw them a great party. All my siblings were in attendance. 2012 is off to a fairly slow start professionally hopefully that's not indicative of what the rest of my year will look like. I'm battling being consistent with my good thoughts and my way of thinking. All I ask is to be in a good place mentally, spiritually, emotionally and professionally. Only through and with my Creator will I achieve this so until next time!

Interesting Fact: The average married couple has sex 58 times per year, or slightly more than once a week. Just two years after marriage, an estimated 20% of couples make love fewer than 10 times in a year.

CHAPTER 9

#Itsthesmallthings

The little things that you miss in the past, can make you miss the most important things in the future.

~ Unknown

As I looked back at my social media postings, I noticed how many pictures I posted with the hashtag #itsthesmallthings, and I thought, I am so blessed. With age comes wisdom, but so does a greater appreciation for the "small things" in life. Over the years there have been countless "small things" my hubby and I have done for each other. So much so, I could write a book solely on that—now that's a blessing. I will share one or two with you:

One day we were cuddling up on the sofa watching mindless reality television; I don't remember the name of the show, but it had to do with cruises, yachts, and room service turning down the beds for their guests. Their process was so simple, yet simultaneously, as we watched it, both Fuji and I acknowledged it immediately. Not only did room service turn down the beds, but they steamed the sheets, warmed the pillow cases, warmed bathroom towels, and placed an animal towel on the bed. Now, I wash and change my sheets regularly, but something rose up within me, so I went straight to the bedroom and did all of the above while Fuji continued watching the program. This all happened before we went to bed, which was approximately ten o'clock. I began cleaning the room, turned down the bed, got newly washed pillowcases out of the closet, and threw them in the dryer for about ten minutes. Once done, I sprayed some of my body spray on the pillows, laying them meticulously across the bed. I neatly organized our side tables and lit his favorite scented candle, placing it on his side. I even sprinkled carpet freshener for an added scent of just-vacuumed freshness. Of course, by the time I started vacuuming, he asked, "Why are you vacuuming so late?" I pretended I did not hear him and carried on with my shenanigans. Once I was done, and I did it all as quickly as I could, I took a bath and put on one of his favorite negligees. So much for watching TV. Off it went. He took a bath and now I will leave it up to you to imagine what happened next! #itsthesmallthings.

That was me doing something small for him. Now here is one example of what he did for me. Since I began writing this book, I've been all of the following and then some: motivated, driven, frustrated, tired, overwhelmed, etc., etc., etc. On this particular day I was beyond stressed. I was having difficulty figuring out some technical issues with my website while preparing dinner and answering homework questions, along with other sidebar conversations. My eldest had practice and my hubby was on his way out and I snapped, yelling, "I can't concentrate with all this going on. Please take them both with you and stay gone for a few hours so I can get my work done." As I'm ushering him and the kids out the door, I turn around, walking back toward the kitchen, only to notice a small gift bag with a card inside. I remember thinking, what is this and how did it get there? I opened the bag and inside was a beautifully wrapped bottle of Daisy perfume by Dolce and Gabbana, along with a card that simply said, "I'm so proud of you and I love you. Love, Fuji." What did I do, you ask? What I do often. I cried! What else should I have done, LOL! Only ten seconds before I had hurried them out of the house so that I could focus and get some work done. #itsthesmallthings.

The small things matter. They make a difference. They change moods. They put things in perspective. Finally, they typically don't cost much but may require some planning—so what? Do it! Not only did he acknowledge that I was stressed and had been stressing for a few days, he took it another step further by adding a nice gesture, purchasing one of my favorite fragrances with a simply stated note attached. I will never forget it!

Here are a few inspirational stories on #itsthesmallthings

I must admit, I admire my own marriage for the team work that we practice. One, because it has NOT always been this way and two, because there was a time that I thought I would NEVER have this type of marriage, even while married. I can remember the first time I realized that what I

*had prayed to God for to deliver in my marriage
had come to fruition. It was the top of 2012, my
father had been diagnosed with dementia and his
live-in girlfriend and his side girlfriend (yes, you
read that right) had known about his illness for
quite some time and had been doing a number on
him financially. Now mind you, my father and
my husband never had a great relationship and at
one point they wanted to have nothing to do with
each other. I had a strained relationship with my
father up until I got wind of how he had been taken
advantage of. I stepped in and gave them both (his
women) their walking papers, and placed my father
in a mental care facility. In the first stages of his
illness, my father was very mean. He would say
some very untrue and nasty things about whomever
was closest to him, mainly ME. Knowing how my
husband and father felt about each other, I didn't
dare ask for help from my husband, but on this
particular day there was no way around it. Having
several meeting and interviews set up for me that
day already, my father fell at the facility he was
currently in and had to be taken to the hospital.
Upon them calling me, I almost had a mental melt
down trying to think about how I was going to get
it all done and see about my own family as well.*

Then my knight and shining armor stepped in and told me to go on and take care of what I needed to take care of; that he would see about my father and our home and not to worry about dinner! To me, asking him was against the odds because of the relationship that was already there - but Glory to God. My husband did not allow that be the deciding factor and he ended up having a very peaceful day with my Dad. When we look back on it, it is a small gesture and even one that most people would say should have been taken in the first place - but to us, it was a milestone, one that bonded us into the team we are today.

~Katrina

One of the special things that my husband Ricky did for me took place about four years ago while I was taking my Series 6 license. The Series 6 exam was one of the most challenging exams of my life. I was preparing for this license for about two months. I was constantly in a bad mood and a couple of times I wanted to give up but Ricky stood by me the entire time constantly motivating me to continue and took care of our son Jolaney in the evenings so I could be able to study. He also helped me by quizzing me every night with flashcards. Thank goodness I passed and I feel that Ricky had a lot to do with my success. He was my rock, a shoulder to cry on, and my punching bag when I was aggravated. Ricky did not complain, not even once. I am so very blessed and could never thank him enough.

~Arlene

"Never again…"

Those words seem to be so definite. But all too often we utter them if not out loud we utter them to ourselves. You see, when you have gone out of your way to make your spouse feel loved and appreciated and they don't respond the way you think they should, deep down inside you may think, "Never again…"

One of the many things I've learned in my almost two decades of marriage is that those words, "never again..." have no place when it comes to showing love in your relationship. Sometimes we seek to look for the grand occasions to go all out, but it's the little things that can mean so much.

If your marriage is anything like ours, there was plenty of time when money was an issue. I've heard that, "necessity is the mother of invention.", "and love will find a way." If that is true, then our love has birth some inventive things over the years.

When you and your spouse need a break from the demands of everyday life, it doesn't have to be a weeklong getaway. It can be an hour long walk ending in an ice cream parlor enjoying your favorite hand dipped ice cream. It could be a slower than normal drive through neighborhoods that are well out of your price range but allows you to dream again an aspire to become the person that can afford those houses WITHOUT forgetting the road you traveled to get there. Maybe even an unplanned picnic in your favorite park. In a spot that was scouted days before so you can catch the perfect sunset. Even an earlier morning walk with the same thing in mind, getting to that spot for the perfect sunrise. Enjoying those little things builds more memories than you would imagine because they are so well crafted and don't require lots of money, but planning. The end result, hopefully your spouse will say "never again… will I doubt your love for me…"

~Cicone

When we first got married, the very first disagreement we had as a couple was over doing the laundry. My husband was complaining that he didn't have any clean underwear to wear because I had not done the laundry. My rebuttal was for him to buy more underwear. Then I told him he if he wanted clean underwear, he could help by doing the laundry. His response was that he didn't know how to do the laundry so I told him to start with whites only. If it's not white, then don't wash it!

One week later, all the white clothes were washed. Then sometime after that, after having a stressful few days at work, I came home and ALL of our dirty laundry was washed, the floors were cleaned *and dinner was cooked! I'll NEVER forget that day and how it made me feel!!! I LOVE my hubby!!!*

~Stacy

One thing my husband did for me that meant the world to me, and I still remember until this day, I was coming out and being emotionally healed from the worst year of my life. My dad, who had been fighting prostate cancer for years, had finally lost the fight and went home to be with the Lord. However, that wasn't the hardest part. It was actually the better part after helping my mother care for him the last 9 months of his life. I saw this man go from being so headstrong, strong-willed, and healthy to a very fragile childlike man. That's who my dad became. It was one of the hardest things I had to ever witness. Although there were many challenges that came with caring for him, I would not change it for the world. At the same time my marriage almost fell apart as we faced the biggest challenge yet. It is by the grace of my heavenly father that we are still together today stronger than ever.

Chapter 9

I was having female problems that led me to having a partial hysterectomy. I was in the hospital for 3 days and in a lot of pain. This man was by my side, never left the hospital until I got discharged. He took care of me, and did everything for me since I was unable to do things for myself. Night after night I would tell him to go home so that he would have a comfortable and restful night but he lovingly refused to leave my side. I was asleep for the most part of the days due to the medications I was taking for all the pain I was in. It would have been totally accepted and justifiable for him to go home, but he wouldn't. I remember waking up out of my sleep, looking off to the side, only to see my husband dosing off, uncomfortable and obviously tired as if he had not slept in days. It was then I knew without a shadow of doubt that this man would stay by my side and care for me, in the same manner and love I cared for my dad. He showed me selfless love and that meant the world to me.

~Rosie

My husband is a very thoughtful, and sensitive man. Everyone that meets him (especially women) always say what a gentleman he is. Since the first day we met he has always been this way. He was raised by older parents, and when I say older I mean when he was in high school his parents were in their sixties, so he has "an old soul".

There are so many things that I can tell you that my husband does that I appreciate, but the one thing that makes me feel like a queen no matter when, no matter where, no matter what the circumstance is, when he picks me up, or we are out moving about, he always always always opens the door for me. It means so much, and makes me feel so respected and special. Now don't get me wrong, I expect this and always have, but it's something about a man that waits for you to emerge from a building while he's standing at the passenger door with it opened, kisses you as if it's a natural part of his being, makes sure you're in and gets in the car and drives off with a smile. It's as if he's been waiting to do this all day. Not only is this done when picking me up from work, it happens when he drops me off, when I'm walking in a building or exiting a building as well. To be honest I can't even tell you the last time I've touched a door since I've been with my husband.

I know it might seem trivial, you might have even been waiting for some big explosive ending from this, but that's it! He does it EVERY DAY, EVERY WHERE we go, and I love it and appreciate it more than he could ever know. The best part about it is, he will do the same for anyone with no problem and I know it, why, because that's just the kind of gentleman he is. That's one of the things I love the most about him. He treats me like the queen I am, which allows me to, without pause, treat him like the king he is.

~Roxanne

Interesting Fact: Marrying younger than age 25 dramatically raises the divorce risk. Also the divorce risk is higher when the woman is much older than the man, though the reverse isn't as a strong factor.

Part Two

TESTIMONIALS, ESSENTIALS, AND WORKBOOK

CHAPTER 10

What Makes A Relationship Successful

There are challenges of human relationships, but I believe there are several key components on how to make that relationship long-lasting, thriving, successful, and meaningful. Having been with the same person for twenty-plus years, I think it's pretty safe to say I know a thing or two about a healthy relationship. I'm by no means claiming that our relationship is perfect, as there is always room for both growth and improvement; however, because I'm still very happy and satisfied with my marriage, I thought I would take the time in the next few chapters to share with you some of the reasons why it worked and continues to work.

My suggestions are very simple and basic, yet many struggle with one, several, most, or even all of these components. No, this was not scientifically proven or tested on one hundred happily married couples, but it has worked for me, so it could certainly work for you as well. As I go through the components, they are placed in order of importance to *me*, somewhat of a guideline, if you will. You need to implement step one before arbitrarily jumping to step five (my opinion).

Even though I'm about to share with you what I think the first step to a successful marriage/relationship is, it doesn't mean it can't be implemented if you've already been together for a number of years. First, I think couples should be friends before lovers. There are so many characteristics or outlooks that could fall under the umbrella of being friends first, so I will address some of the more obvious aspects.

By being each other's best friend first—BFF, as today's society likes to refer to it—you will discover authentically who this person is. The key to becoming friends before lovers is being *authentic*. Meeting someone for the first time, we sometimes put on "our best face," and that's all right, but we have to be careful not to take it to the extreme. Being authentic allows you the opportunity to meet the "real" person; this person is not pretending to be someone he or she is not and could possibly be seen as trustworthy. This is the person friends and family know and see on a daily basis. At the end of the day, isn't that the person you'd like to meet before engaging in a deeper and more committed relationship? Cautiously observing another person over a period of time reveals a great deal. I'm certain you've heard people say, "If only I'd paid attention to the signs," they may not have chosen the mate they did, eventually ending in divorce. All the signs were there; you simply chose to ignore them. Listen, you've got to be able to be yourself, that is, act a fool, pick your toenails, use the bathroom with the door open, walk around with your hair unkempt, pass gas, burp, whatever "acting a fool" means to you. Yes, the last two were gross, but I'm just trying to make a point. In other words, don't do what I did at Denny's: eat two shrimps when I really wanted to eat the entire plate. You've got to be able to be you!

Personal example: Before Fuji and I officially began dating, I remember going to Pizza Hut on South Beach. We sat down and placed our order. Once the food got there we served ourselves and started eating. I had cheese all over my mouth—didn't care. I had barbeque meat stuck between my teeth—didn't care. I reached over into his plate and took food off of his plate—didn't care and neither did he. Of course I cleaned up, but when I say "I just didn't care," I mean I was going to be myself, be normal. So what if I got cheese on my face? That's why they made napkins, SMH! It was a far cry from eating at Denny's, right? We were really good friends.

Assessment: No matter where you are in your relationship, was this component ever applied? If yes, great. If not, do you see or understand why it may now make a difference or could have made a difference?

Quote: *"The best kind of relationship is when they're not only your lover, but your best friend too."* ~ *Author Unknown.*

Notes:

_____

_____

_____

_____

_____

_____

_____

_____

_____

_____

_____

_____

_____

_____

_____

_____

_____

Another cool quality about becoming friends first is learning what special interests, likes, or dislikes the person may have. Once you've become friends, you make all sorts of awesome discoveries. Whether good or bad, they are being made. It's during this phase you could learn if he or she has any fetishes. If Fuji had a crazed foot fetish, for example, such as that he liked sucking on toes, that might have been a problem for me, as I didn't start liking my feet until just last week (smile). I'm not saying it would have been a deal breaker, but we would really need to address it at some point.

One of my girlfriends has a male friend who is very much into her and has been "courting" her for about three years. During the three years, they have been unknowingly building and strengthening their friendship (BFF status) before becoming lovers. He's expressed to her one of his "likes," which is to buy fresh flowers for his home weekly. My response to her was, that depicts love, kindness, sensitivity, even a positive attitude or outlook on life. I personally love fresh flowers and appreciate the joy it brings me, and I gather it does something similar for him.

Personal example: As friends, I knew Fuji was into cars, specifically Corvettes, because he had one, and, growing up with three brothers and a dad who was also a mechanic, I too had interests in cars. This was one awesome commonality, especially for him. Guys like nothing more than girls digging what they dig, but I would never fake it. Remember, be *authentic*.

Assessment: At what point in the relationship were your discoveries made? Were they ever made?

Quote: *"Be yourself, everyone else is taken." ~ Author Unknown.*

Notes:

_____
_____
_____
_____
_____
_____
_____
_____
_____
_____
_____
_____
_____
_____
_____

You know that old adage "the way to a man's heart is through his stomach"? I know some of you may not like to cook and don't want to learn how to cook, but how about we compromise a bit? Hear me out. During this stage there's a good probability you will have gone out to eat a time or two; whether it's at a restaurant or a home-cooked meal, you will have shared a dining experience. Undoubtedly, conversations revolving around favorite foods will come up. The discovery will be made. Once you become lovers and are no longer friends, this now becomes an advantage.

Personal example: I learned early on that Fuji loved white rice and red beans with some sort of protein, especially cooked and prepared by his mother. By the time we were dating I made sure I got plenty of one-on-one lessons from his favorite cook. Now, I make the meanest *arroz blanco con habichuelas con chuletas* (translation: white rice and red beans with pork chops) his pallet has ever had.

Assessment: Cooking may or may not be a deal breaker for some couples. If it is, is it something you are willing to compromise on? No one is suggesting you prepare seven-course meals daily, but what about occasionally preparing *his or her* favorite dish? Trust me, this goes a long way!

Quote: "*The only real stumbling block is fear of failure. In cooking you've got to have a what-the-hell attitude.*" ~ *Julia Child.*

Notes:

_____

_____

_____

_____

_____

_____

_____

_____

_____

_____

_____

_____

_____

_____

_____

_____

_____

How important are *family* and *culture* to you? They are very important to me. As friends, this may be one of the first differences you encounter. If you grew up in the Caribbean, as I did, then you understood the "Caribbean" culture. Here in America, there are a myriad of cultures, and more and more people are dating outside of their cultures. Again, this could be a deal breaker for some, while it's not for others. As part of other people's cultures, you will also witness how they interact with their family members. Were they raised in a single family home? What are their temperaments like? Are they loving, and is he or she a momma's boy/daddy's girl? All of these things can be determining factors as to whether or not you should become a couple. Some habits you may be willing to accept, while others maybe not so much. Spend time getting to know not only the person, but maybe his or her family and friends as well. I always learned something new about Fuji whenever we visited or spent time with his cousins, aunts, and uncles. To this day I make some pretty interesting discoveries.

Personal example: Culturally I have learned that Puerto Ricans are far more expressive and loving than we are (Jamaicans). Growing up, we knew within our family we were loved, but it was never expressed verbally, and if it was, it was rare. With Fuji's family, they told each other "I love you" several times a day, and they hugged and kissed regularly too. Honestly, at first I found it annoying because it was something I was not used to, but over time I accepted and even adopted it.

Assessment: What will you or won't you accept from a culture other than your own? How important is that to you?

Quote: *"Preservation of one's own culture does not require contempt or disrespect for other cultures." ~ Cesar Chavez.*

Notes:

_____

_____

_____

_____

_____

_____

_____

_____

_____

_____

_____

_____

_____

CHAPTER 11

Respect: If You Want It, You've Got To Give It

What is respect and why is it vital? *Mutual respect* is the footing of a loving relationship. It's a combination of gratitude, admiration, and acknowledgment of a person being worth something. At times it may appear obscure; some people get it, while others don't. In this day and age, respect is practically nonexistent and sometimes confused with fear. Women and young girls allow men and boys to speak to them inappropriately and, at times, justify their behavior, probably all out of fear. I'm here to tell you that it's 100 percent unacceptable, it's not necessary, and I've never read anywhere (and I'm a pretty avid reader) that treating others disrespectfully is a sign of love or affection. Not only is it degrading and cruel, but it can be damaging and lead to a host of destructive self-image issues, such as low self-esteem and lack of confidence. Here's a perfect example of that:

My fifteen-year marriage ended because of the downward spiral effect a lack of respect had on it. It started with name calling, which led to verbal abuse, eventually causing me to suffer from low self-esteem. As a result, I ended up in psychotherapy for three years. I was at the bottom of the barrel, where I felt trapped and helpless. What took years to build was destroyed with hurtful, derogatory words, and once they were said we could never take them back. Apologizing repeatedly never took away the pain or the mark that was left because of those cutting words. I would never enter into another relationship disrespecting my mate or allowing him to disrespect me. Without respect, there's no mutual affection for each other. My advice: think about what it is you are willing to accept, how you want to be treated, and how you will treat the other person. ~ Anonymous

To get respect, you must first give it, but know that it starts with you. Before we can truly respect another human being, we have to learn how to respect ourselves. Know that you deserve respect, but it's up to you to set and demand the standard.

Once this has been established, you will quickly realize that disrespect has no place in your life.

Some people witness disrespect their entire lives, from the time they are kids, and as a result they later become disrespectful adults. If this is the case in your relationship, then it's important that it's acknowledged, then you must take action and set the tone. It may take some time to correct, but if the relationship has value, then it may be worth it for both parties to make a conscious decision to work on establishing and correcting the behavior.

Women, never go against your morals to impress or keep a man. First of all, a little secret, a real man—a good man—hates that. Secondly, if you're doing something you would not normally do, then he's probably not worth it. So to that I say, abort ship and keep sailing. In addition, don't feel the need to "give up the cookie" too quickly or easily. Believe it or not, this too is a sign to the opposite sex of how you feel about yourself and your level of self-love and self-worth. Steve Harvey calls it "the ninety-day rule," I believe: when starting a new relationship, wait ninety days before sex. It's not about playing hard to get. If a man is impressed with what you have to offer otherwise and he's clearly noticed that you are displaying a great deal of self-respect, he will keep coming back for more. On the contrary, and most importantly, men hate being disrespected or emasculated. Men are just as insecure as women, so when the opportunity presents itself, don't be afraid to openly flaunt how much you respect him. In turn you are winning him over. Both the love and respect he has for you will in fact increase and in time be reciprocated. Bottom line: men respect women who love and respect themselves.

Respect is paramount in a happy relationship. As far as successful relationships, including my own, the most successful ones I've encountered were those who treated each other with great respect. Like trust, this goes a long way and is imperative in the foundation of the relationship.

Personal example: Early in our relationship my husband and I had a major disagreement. I called him an inappropriate name, and unfortunately he heard me. His response was, "I've never disrespected you. Please don't ever do that again." He was right! He's never called me a name; therefore, he does not deserve to be called one either. Additionally, he set the tone and the precedent by saying, "Please don't ever do that again." Trust me, it's never, ever happened again in the two decades we've been together. In some households it's accepted and becomes a part of the routine. It's second nature—how very sad! I'm truly hoping it's not part of yours. Another thing we don't do is swear at each other.

Don't get me wrong, occasionally I might lose it, but it's never directed toward him. Remember, he set the tone long ago. Cursing, name calling, and dropping f-bombs all over the place are big no-nos in our house!

Assessment: Can you say that you and your partner are equally respectful of each other? It doesn't matter how many times lack of respect happens. Once is one time too many. Set the tone!

Quote: *"Don't lower your* worth *just to keep someone in your life. Find someone that is* willing *to give you what you're worth."* ~ *Author Unknown.*

Notes:

_____

_____

_____

_____

_____

_____

_____

_____

_____

_____

_____

_____

_____

CHAPTER 12

Trusting Your Spouse Or Your Mate

Relationships should be based on partners being honest and truthful from the very beginning. Trust is something that takes years to build but mere seconds to destroy. If you've worked that hard to maintain or to gain something so important and valuable in your relationship, why jeopardize it with betrayal, dishonesty, and lies? The ramifications of lying are so heavy and often hurtful, it's sometimes difficult to survive them. Not only that, who has the time to lie? It takes so much work to remember what you said and to keep the snowball going. Like Sweet Brown says, "Ain't nobody got time for that...Lord Jesus, there's a fire!"

Earlier I stated that the truth may sting during an argument, but it also provides a sense of security. It creates a safe environment for growth. How do you build trust? First, start by showing you are trustworthy with little things. Show the other person you are capable of keeping things between the two of you. Over time these little things become bigger things, and the other person then finds you more and more upright. Secondly, trust is a two-way street; therefore, you must also allow yourself to be vulnerable. Share personal and intimate details about yourself with your partner, and hopefully he or she will do the same. Moreover, building trust also means spending time together. Technology and social media have interrupted bonding time between couples. Nothing should ever replace that one-on-one time if you are looking to build trust.

Once the trust is broken, can it be repaired? This really depends on the individual and the circumstance. For instance, infidelity (one of the many things people lie about) for many is hard to recover from for multiple reasons. The individual who was being deceived starts questing everything, such as:

∽ Is he really doing what he said he was doing?

∽ Did he really go to work today or is he spending it with her?

∽ While making love, is he thinking of her?

∽ Who is he talking to on the phone?

And the list goes on and on. How long are you willing to second-guess everything the person does? This could create an entirely new set of problems in addition to trust issues. Again, what are you willing to tolerate? In this case I strongly suggest seeking professional counseling from a reliable and reputable source, such as a psychologist or a pastor. There are countless success stories about relationships that survive infidelity, believe it or not, but it's just not a chance I'm willing to take. I have too much at stake and too much to lose. When I stop to think about the devastation it would cause my sons and other family members, it's simply not worth it.

Trust does not solely apply to infidelity. People lie about the following and then some:

∽ Financial issues

- How much money they make

- How much debt they are in

- Their gambling/spending habits

~ Sex and intimacy

- How good the partner is

- Having fantasies about someone other than their mate or spouse

- Being satisfied

- The number of partners they've had; having unprotected sex

~ Relational

- Their level of commitment

- Their feelings for past lovers; maybe they are still interested

- Whether they are in love or not

- Why they can't spend time with you

~ Negative behaviors

- Smoking, doing drugs

- Gambling

- Alcohol use

∾ Insecurities

- Jealousy

- Family and friends—they make them out to be better than they really are so you'll like them

- Health, age, weight

These are just some of the things that people falsify for whatever reason, but at some point during the relationship the truth is typically revealed. Being honest and upfront from the start saves so much heartache, pain and ill will. My advice: don't do it, instead talk it out. Work on those communication skills. Give your mate the benefit of the doubt and address the issue at hand. There's no real reason why the truth should hurt if handled correctly. Remember, it's not what you say, but how you say it. It's all in the delivery. A simple example of this: *Option A*: "I really hate that blue shirt you're wearing." *Option B*: "I'm not a huge fan of that blue shirt, but the green one really makes your eyes pop." *Option A* is so harsh and aggressive. It almost seems hateful. *Option B* is so subtle he or she won't even focus on the fact that you hate the blue shirt but instead will hear that you noticed that his or her eyes popped when wearing the green one. Great technique, give it a try!

Personal example: As seemingly insignificant as this example may seem, over time it could have escalated into something greater. I love to cook, especially Fuji's favorite dishes. However, sometimes I like to try new things. There's a chicken recipe that my sister-in-law makes with stir-fried vegetables, but the secret is in the sweet, tangy sauce. This dish, served over white rice, is simply scrumptious. The first time Fuji had it, he said he liked it—I loved it. Besides that, it was so easy to make, and on those days that I don't feel like being in the kitchen all day, this is the meal to prepare. Seriously, from start to finish it probably takes 20 minutes—ideal, right? I began serving this meal probably once a week with my busy schedule, and finally one day I said, "Isn't this great, honey?" He responded, "Yeah, it's really good," but the expression on his face did not match what came out of his mouth (laugh out loud). I laughed and said, "Honey, if and whenever I make something, don't lie about liking it, because I will only continue to make it, and I want you enjoy what I make for dinner every time you eat it." He is such a pleaser and goes out of his way not to hurt my feelings, but I'd rather know upfront whether or not he likes what I cook! Again, put those communication skills to work.

Assessment: How important is trust to you? Where does it fall in your relationship? Has it ever been broken or compromised?

Quote: *"When it comes to relationships, remaining faithful is never an option but a priority. Loyalty is everything." ~ Author Unknown.*

Notes:

_____

_____

_____

_____

_____

_____

_____

_____

_____

_____

_____

_____

_____

CHAPTER 13

Without Communication Your Relationship Can Perish

Communication is the art of *effectively* exchanging information with each other, saying what we feel, being clear about what is being conveyed, and listening attentively to what is being expressed. I know that seems like a mouthful, but it's a skill that is necessary for creating and preserving loving relationships. Some will have to work at it harder than others.

When I was a child, my parents did not fight or argue regularly. They had their disagreements like most couples do, but how they resolved them is information we were never privy to, and rightfully so—we were kids. As an adult, looking back, having spoken to my mom, and now as a parent myself, I see that my parents were terrible communicators. There was a lot of walking away, holding in feelings, and not saying how they both felt about a situation, which I'm sure over the years led to resentment. How could it not? Somehow they have managed to get through it and have been married for almost fifty years. Sadly, as kids, I cannot recall our parents regularly saying those three simple words that everyone should hear often and daily, "I love you." Even though this was normal for me, I knew without a shadow of a doubt that both my parents loved us unconditionally and more than anything in the world. They showed their love by their actions. Was it right? It wasn't wrong, because that was all they knew. It's how they were raised. It's how they were shown love.

My dad was raised by his grandmother. He was abandoned by both his parents as a toddler. My dad is almost seventy years old (born in 1947), and it was only ten years ago that I forced him to start saying "I love you." I expressed to him the importance of saying those three words. It was such a difficult thing for him to do. He struggled with it but I understood. I'm so happy that he can now say it without difficulty.

My mom (born in 1945) was raised by both parents with her six siblings, and she's told me on numerous occasion there was very little love shown or expressed from the time she was a child all the way into adulthood. Like my dad, she did not know how to verbally express it either. You would think it would have been different because she was raised with both of her parents, but this is why I say it was our culture. Nonetheless, It was definitely easier to get my mom to say "I love you." I'm not sure why that is, but it was.

Was it enough in how they showed us love? At the time it was because it was what we knew. Would it be enough now? Absolutely not! Saying "I love you" verbally is imperative, and not just between couples, but between the children, other family members, and friends. Verbally expressing your love to your loved ones is not the same thing as showing it in your actions. The purpose of language is to impart information or explain something to someone. While that is the purpose of language, to communicate requires dialogue, which is language between two or more people.

Communication is an area Fuji and I struggled with severely for many years. Note, I said *struggled* with, not *are struggling* with—thank goodness. I do believe women are better communicators than men, but that doesn't mean that they can't or they shouldn't try. Perhaps it's just different. "Men compartmentalize their feelings, but women remember everything," says Christiane Northrup, MD. Yes, we do!

Here are some simple phrases that you should be comfortable saying:

∾ I love you.

∾ I love it when you _____.

∾ I don't like it when you _____.

∾ I'm wrong and I'm sorry.

∾ Tell me how you're feeling.

∾ What is it you are feeling?

∾ How can I fix this?

∾ What will it take to make things better?

∾ How can I help you?

∾ I enjoy/don't enjoy this in the bedroom.

∾ I feel like _____.

Communicating the above should not be done via technology or social media forums. Use your language to express all of the above verbally and face to face when feasible. I believe I've said this repeatedly throughout the book: it's not what you say to the person, but how you say it. It's all in the delivery. Choose your words wisely to ensure you are articulating what you are in fact meaning to say. Do you know how many problems you would solve or inadvertently avoid if you applied all of the above to your relationship? Try it!

In order to make that connection, here is a list of guidelines you should follow. They are all demonstrative of a healthy and loving relationship.

- Never assume.

- Don't mind read.

- Don't predetermine the outcome.

- Compliment in public, reprimand in private.

- Express joyous feelings and thoughts.

- Give gifts randomly, not only on special occasions.

∾ Never negate a person's feeling because it's not real for you; it's his or her experience.

∾ Touch, hold, and hug frequently.

∾ Respect each other's space.

Personal example: Without a doubt Fuji and I struggled with this for the first several years of our young marriage. It was very difficult, as I would always freely express my thoughts and my feelings as Dr. Northrup suggested we as women do. He was quite the contrary, and it caused me to be frustrated, bitter, and even at times angry, until eventually a combination of things happened. I realized, and in part accepted, that he wasn't as expressive as I was. However, instead of getting angry, I would repeatedly tell him how I felt and how it would make me feel if he expressed himself to me, regardless of whether I was in agreement or not with what he had to say. I think he was concerned about hurting my feelings, to which I in turn said, "I'm a big girl, I can handle it, and if I can't, I will get over it." I had to convince him that it was OK to express himself to me regardless of the outcome, even if it stung a bit. This was a combination of the skills mentioned above.

Assessment: On a scale of one to ten, ten being great communication between you and your mate, how would you rate your communication? Does it make you angry and cause resentment? Try the skills mentioned earlier.

Quote: *"Assumptions are the termites of relationships."* ~ *Henry Winkler.*

Notes:

_____

_____

_____

_____

_____

_____

_____

_____

_____

_____

_____

_____

_____

CHAPTER 14

The Importance Of Sex To A Marriage

Physical intimacy was created by God, and it was intended to be something beautiful to bring us joy and pleasure, even though our culture has made it muddy and distorted.

Sex doesn't begin in the bedroom; in fact it begins prior to it. Sex is a package that should be beautifully wrapped (with love, kind gestures, affirmation, walks and talks together, helping with chores, helping with the kids, honor, respect, trust, communication), and when opened it should be explosive (passion and fireworks in the bedroom).

Ever wonder why in the earlier stages of your relationship sex was great, you couldn't get enough of it, but as time progressed your "great sex life" became a "good sex life," which eventually lead to a "hardly ever having sex life" and finally to a "no sex life"? Part of that reason is the package was not properly wrapped and presented. Early in the relationship the qualities listed above in the previous chapters were perhaps never present or weren't established going forward. Sadly, many of them were most likely even taken for granted.

I love talking to women about relationships and their sex lives—not intimate details, of course, but about sex in general, and what I've learned through these conversations and personal experiences is that sex is an assembly of things, a package. My point was proven in a blog I wrote and published August 11, 2014. It had been shared more than 135 times as of September 12, 2014:

> When it comes to relationships, what do women really want? What does it take to make them happy? The answer is...*not much!* The things that make women happy in a relationship are more simplistic and common than you may think. Sometimes I believe men overthink this concept, so I'm here to share with you those five things that your woman wants and needs:

1. ***Quality time.*** Women who are unhappy in their relationships spend less than five minutes per

day with their spouses. Quality time means at least thirty minutes or more of continuous time with your spouse, date night included. Turn off the TV, the phones, the computer, and all other electronic devices. Instead, possibly brew some tea, cuddle up on the sofa, massage each other's feet, and talk about each other's day.

2. ***Feeling rescued and protected.*** Even though I'm extremely independent and know I can do anything I want to, it doesn't mean I want to run my household or "wear the pants in the relationship." We all want our very own Superman. Even though there are many things that we, my hubby and I, take turns doing and share in the responsibility for, there are some things I just don't want to do, such as take out the trash, schedule oil changes for my car, or go house hunting on my own. Men, take the initiative and do these things for your woman. Trust me, she will love and appreciate you for it. We want to feel protected and coddled, not smothered and covered!

3. ***Being understood.*** We can tell when you are tuned in or out. Not only is being tuned out rude, it's insensitive and hurtful. It implies you don't care and would rather be doing something else.

Listen attentively when your wife wants to talk. If it's important to her, it should be important enough for you to listen.

4. ***Feeling appreciated.*** Men, take the time to not only tell your wife that you appreciate her, but show her as well. You know we wear many hats and oftentimes wear multiple hats without thinking about it, so please tell/show us that you value what we do, such as cooking, cleaning, chauffeuring the kids back and forth, etc., etc., etc., etc. Place a single rose on my pillow with a simple note that says "thank you." This move is priceless!

5. ***Kind gestures.*** Sending your wife a spontaneous text message saying something like "you're truly the love of my life" might earn you brownie points in the bedroom later that night. Any sort of physical touch could also spark the flames—a hug, kissing, and a soft tap on the derriere, all of which only take seconds to do! The rose on the pillow might too, I'll add, if you missed it the first time.

The response and feedback I received from this blog was mind blowing. It's as if I hit the nail on the head!

Chapter 14

Now that we've accomplished "packaging" sex, it's time to open it, the "explosion." I left sex for last because once all the other components are in place, such as trust and communication, your sex life should be vibrant and robust. *Trust:* you trust your partner enough to allow yourself to be free—free from judgment and inhibitions. *Communicate:* now you are able to express your likes and dislikes in the bedroom and what feels good or what doesn't.

The secret to great sex, or, if you prefer, lovemaking:

∾ *Don't rush it.* For younger couples, men in particular, take your time. Be selfless. Make sure your wife is equally enjoying the experience.

∾ *To be in the mood or not.* If you were to wait until both parties were in the mood, your sex life would be practically null and void. If one person is not in the mood, it doesn't mean he or she can't be *persuaded.* You've already learned to trust and communicate in the bedroom; now add patience and creativity there as well.

∾ *Know that preorgasm is the best part.* Think about this: sex is most pleasurable and pleasing *during* the act. How many times have you whispered to yourself during the act, "I don't want this to end," because you know that once the big *O* occurs, the party is over and the physical pleasure ends?

I'll share with you one final article I came across, written by a female. The blog is entitled "5 Reasons You Should Have Sex with Your Husband Every Night."

It is so much blasted fun. Seriously. Why are we so quick to refuse the good things in life? We will slog through our children's algebra homework, do Zumba in public and pluck the hair from our body ONE PIECE AT A TIME. But tell a girl to have sex every night and she looks at you like you are crazy, An orgasm? Every night? What do I look like? A Nymphomaniacal Super Woman? Where is the logic in that? Are we really too busy doing dishes to participate in an activity that is so good it has inspired genius (that saucy Shakespeare) and changed history (Okay, Helen of Troy, we get it.

You were superhot)? My goodness, what a crazy way to live. Ladies, did it ever occur to you (to us!) that we should have sex because WE DESERVE IT? Yeah, you deserve it.

I'm just glad to know I'm not the only woman who feels this way (smile). It also goes without saying that as you get older, it becomes more about quality versus quantity.

Personal example: We are not lacking in this area at all. I often wonder how is it possible that the last time we made love was better than the time before that. I would also like to add that we are both eager to please each other; after all, it's a two-way street. I am *still* so very much in love with this man, and sex plays an essential role in that. It's not just about the physical aspect, but the emotional existence that is created during sex. It's a beautiful thing! For kicks and giggles I keep track of the number of times we make love every month. I have a personal sex chart on my calendar and I will say that every month is quite colorful (wink, wink).

Assessment: How often are you having sex? Are you both on the same page with the number of times you have sex? Your mate's response will surprise you I'm sure. What are you striving for, good sex or great sex?

Quote: *"We are all born sexual creatures, thank God, but it's a pity so many people despise and crush this natural gift." ~ Marilyn Monroe.*

Notes:

_____

_____

_____

_____

_____

_____

_____

_____

_____

_____

_____

_____

_____

_____

_____

_____

_____

CHAPTER 15

101 Tips For A Successful Relationship

Writing this book was challenging, at times overly demanding, however the journey was priceless and I am glad I saw it through to the end. I truly hope you found value in it. It's not meant to solve all of your relationship concerns, but provide possible solutions to some of your problems or questions. I think if people invested the time, go back to the basic and stop trying to re-invent the wheel, apply what worked for many years ago with class and finesse, that ideal relationship could be achieved.

With that said, special thanks to the people listed below who submitted their personal tips on what's important in having a successful relationship.

1. *Tara ~ "ALWAYS ALWAYS ALWAYS find quiet moments to be alone. Life gets in the way. Kids get in the way. If you don't find time to be alone, trouble steps in and pulls you apart."*

2. *Dynell ~ "God in the center of everything, and a commitment to accept each other for who we are, flaws and all."*

3. *Michelle ~ "I would say communication is the key, always express how you feel to each other, be a great listener."*

4. *Denise ~ "We pray for each other, and we pray together. Yes, out loud and every day. Even if we're upset or have had a disagreement, we hold hands and pray over everything!"*

5. *Diana ~ "Greet your man at the door as if you haven't seen him in months."*

6. *Melinda ~ "Never go to bed mad at each other!"*

7. *Roxanne* ~ *"Make your spouse your best friend, have lots of passion and sex. At all cost never break the trust, keep your marriage between you and your spouse."*

8. *Cicone* ~ *"Love is more than a feeling. Love is sacrificial and gives for the greater good. (John 3:16) It really shines brightest when times are hard and you want to give up. Love then stands up and fights for*

9. *Vivian* ~ *"Fighting will happen...just fight fair, stick to the topic and never go personal. Don't ever hold back an apology if you feel you're wrong."*

10. *Carol* ~ *"You have to give up your right sometimes just to have a little peace."*

11. *Irene* ~ *"Have fun and laugh together. It takes away the pressure and stresses of parenting and daily life. Once you're laughing and having fun enjoying each other's company, everything else seems to be more fun and playful!"*

12. *Mitchell* ~ *"Respect and love one another as if were your last day on earth together."*

13. Aprille ~ *"Be willing to explore all sexual fantasies and intimate desires! Don't lose the physical connection between the two of you."*

14. Danielle ~ *"Aim to be happy, rather than to be right. The pursuit of proving your point and being "right" can rob you of your happiness. So choose your battles wisely!"*

15. Jerry ~ *"My wife Aysha and I have committed to going to a marriage conference or marriage retreat once a year. This helps us stay accountable to our marriage covenant and to feed our marriage with what God intended for our marriage."*

16. Kelli ~ *"Make sure your partner is your true friend. Get to know your friend. We accept so much from our friends and love them despite their flaws. If we try to be lovers first we have no patience with them or their short comings."*

17. Lakecia ~ *"I have been with my spouse for 22 years and the technique I use is loving yourself first in order to love your spouse unconditionally."*

18. Christina (Tina) ~ *"Being "truthful"...even if it hurts. Liars never gain respect once exposed."*

19. *Beverly ~ "Share in each other's interest whatever it may be. Also listen to each other not just hear each other but listen."*

20. *Kiana ~ "Remember your anniversary is for both of you and can be planned by either of you. Also don't force him to do it as a declaration of his love to you."*

21. *Gwenn ~ "Live in the now! Not the 'Let's wait until tonight.'*

22. *Kalifah ~ "Trust is earned and built simultaneously! Never assume anything, because what you "think" may be a problem, could very well be just a problem for you - not for BOTH!"*

23. *Trina ~ "Continue to seek opportunities for new experiences to have fun with each other. You weren't busy and boring when you first started dating so don't be that way now! Keep the fun alive!"*

24. *Jessica ~ "Learn to say, "I'm sorry" and mean it!"*

25. *Jo-Ann ~ "Marry only in The Lord." 1 Corinthians 7:39*

26. *Rosie ~ "It pleases God and he commands us to respect our husbands. In growing spiritually it then becomes easier for us to extend grace and forgiveness to our spouses. As we practice that, we will get that in return as we will need respect, grace, and forgiveness as well."*

27. *Emmett ~ "Maturity in a relationship is not when you start speaking big things to impress. It's when we understand how what we say makes your mate feel!"*

28. *Tara ~ "Every year plan a romantic getaway."*

29. *Silmary ~ "Communication and trust is key to a healthy and successful relationship. Marriage takes work. It's not something that you have to stop working on just because you feel comfortable. Always remember to make special time for your partner."*

30. *Sandra ~ "Always respect your partner's opinion even when you do not agree with it."*

31. *Denise ~ "Work on yourself far more than you work on the relationship. It's a win-win!"*

32. *Nicole ~ "Love is a choice, and keeping your "emotional love tank" full is just as important as the physical needs in a relationship. Words of affirmation, quality time together, and physical touch are what makes a relationship succeed."*

33. *Patrecia ~ "The key to any marriage is communication."*

34. *Heather ~ "Keep Christ at the center."*

35. *Debbie ~ "After 35 years of marriage I'm so happy I didn't give up during the hard times. The best times come after the hard times if you learn from them! My faith in family values kept me focused and I thank God every day that I stayed with my husband!"*

36. *Jeremy ~ "Choose a (God-fearing) mate based on who they are right now, not who they 'have the potential to be'. There is a good chance they will never turn into the person you were 'hoping they would become', whereby creating a performance based relationship."*

37. *Edwin ~ "Remember to compliment her to the point she still feels you are attracted to her."*

38. Nadine ~ *"Don't tear each other down with your words or actions, but build each other up even through the hard times."*

39. Laura Faye ~ *"Be who you are from day one. Do the things that you always did from the very first date. This is the only way for it to work. Set proper expectations. If you are a man who does not bring flowers, then do not bring them from the start."*

40. Martin – *"The one commonality that I have witnessed in every type of successful relationship is for both parties to selflessly begin from within so that each are enabled to give to the other the core comprehensiveness of each to the other."*

41. Tosh ~ *"Be attentive. Show respect. Communicate. Laugh. Take care of yourself."*

42. Garrick ~ *"Everyday both persons should ask the other, what I can do today to make you happy?"*

43. Deon ~ *"Both parties should put God first, their significant other second, and themselves last."*

44. Pastor Raymond ~ *"Keep God in your marriage. Be open. Never have a relationship where communication*

is not vital because communication is the life to a healthy and successful marriage. Support one another. Build up one another. And spend time with each other."

45. *Tangela ~ "Always be true to yourself. If you are not true to yourself how can you be true to your mate?"*

46. *Octavia ~ "Say thank you. Do you ever notice how polite you are to strangers if you drop something and they pick it up, but we forget those things when it's our spouse? Be grateful for all the little things."*

47. *Leslie ~ "Always treat your wife like a woman and your husband like a man, respectfully, no matter the circumstance."*

48. *Mario ~ "Know yourself. The better you know yourself the more honest you can be with what you want, with yourself, and your partner."*

49. *Michelle ~ "Marriage is a business, you have to work at it... work in it...work on it...24/7! I have a job I enjoy and I work diligently. However, I have a marriage and I love every aspect of it.*

50. *Derek ~ "Share a laugh every day. If you are busy smiling, you have no time to argue."*

51. *Dezetta ~ Eccl 4:12 tells us "...a threefold cold cannot quickly be torn apart." If we always strive to apply this Bible principles, then when problems do arise it will be easier to work through."*

52. *Paula ~ "Marriage is hard work! Don't let anybody fool you into thinking it's a fairy tale. If you're selfish, immature, always in your feelings and not spiritually grounded, you might want to stay single."*

53. *Stacy ~ "If you put God first and always try to compromise with your partner, life will be so much smoother."*

54. *Brenda ~ "Even though you are a couple you are still two individuals. Continue to be you. One day when the new is no longer cute you may blame the other for changing you."*

55. *Myrna B. ~ "Just be there to listen! Be all ears and get off of any device when your husband gets home!"*

56. *Romey ~ "Be your partners "safe place."*

Chapter 15

57. *Amelia ~ "Make each other laugh whenever possible! When a "discussion" is getting heated, I just break out with something funny that will make us forget what we were even arguing about! Laughter solves just about any argument!"*

58. *Charmion ~ "Know when to keep quiet and hold your peace. Being right is not always as important as we may think."*

59. *Bianca ~ "Quality time."*

60. *Sophia ~ "It may seem cliché, but relationships will not succeed without compromise, mutual respect, and most of all, love for each other."*

61. *Maria ~ "When you get upset with your significant other, remember the reason(s) you fell in love with them in the first place. For instance, when my husband gets me in that 'not so happy' place, I think back to his genuine and pure heart, and how he always has my back."*

62. *Angie ~ "Always try to make your partner happy. It sounds very simple but if a wife focuses on her husband's happiness and vice versa both will be happy and will feel fulfilled in the relationship."*

63. Karen ~ *"Give your mate a little space to unwind."*

64. Phillip ~ *"Kiss your spouse every day! No matter the circumstance! Good times, bad times, boring times or even in the middle of an argument. A kiss is very personal and it is the one thing that you can do every day, no matter the mood."*

65. Mae ~ *"Trust and honesty is pretty basic and key to any relationship but the love and dedication that each other offers is what makes the relationship last as long as they make it."*

66. Terri ~ *"Friendship is the most important part of a marriage. A true friendship will last a lifetime. My spouse is my very best friend."*

67. Latoya ~ *"A successful marriage is built on trust, loyalty, and communication I have been with my husband since middle school and we have four beautiful children we enjoy spending time together we do dinner three times a month to keep up with each other's opinions etc."*

68. Bob ~ *"Commit to kissing each other every day! Not a peck on the forehead or cheek, but a face to face smack on the lips! This kind of consistent connection between*

a husband and wife helps keep a level of togetherness, even through difficult times."

69. *Brittany ~ "Obedience to God's word. Every marriage hits a breaking point. At that point, the world will encourage you to move on. Trusted friends and family will tell you that you have done all you can to make it work, but surely God doesn't want you to be unhappy. If you go directly to His word, however, you will see that nowhere in the bible is God focused on our happiness. He does explicitly say that he hates divorce, and that marriage is a covenant not to be broken. The hardest decision you will make in your marriage is to stay when your heart is telling you to leave, but the bible says "the heart is deceitful above all things." Staying and choosing to live by God's word will lead you to something better than the fleeting emotion of happiness; you will experience a deep, lasting, spiritual joy. Being willing to sacrifice your temporary happiness will lead you to a more fulfilling marriage than you ever thought possible."*

70. *Gwen (**bonus**) ~ "Stay children at heart! Stay in for Saturday morning cartoons, get the water guns out...LAUGH."*

71. *Kalifah (**bonus**) ~ "Learn to listen, openly, and completely. A two-way street that is often jaywalked.*

Couples should always respect their partner enough to listen to their ideas, opinions or even complaints.

72. Nancy (**bonus**) ~ *"Giving each other space."*

73. Trina (**bonus**) ~ *"Take turns every week planning date night!"*

74. Jessica (**bonus**) ~ *"When God joins two people together, it's with purpose; remember your purpose!"*

75. Jo-Ann (**bonus**) ~ *"When you see red flags, don't ignore them. Actions usually always speak louder than words."*

76. Emmett (**bonus**) ~ *"The practical message is to encourage you to look at the relationships in your lives and ask the important question. I am developing my relationship, I am striving to secure our foundation and I am a good influence to our friends and to my mate."*

77. Sandra (**bonus**) ~ *"Always have your partners back even when they are wrong. Wait until you two are alone and tell him that he was wrong never in public."*

78. Denise (**bonus**) ~ *"Choose to meet your partners needs as a reflection of your love."*

79. *Nicole (**bonus**) ~ "Men want to be respected, and respect motivates your man. The power of your words alone build your man up or down. Your attitude not your aptitude will determine your altitude."*

80. *Kenia ~ "Be transparent and have no secrets."*

81. *Patrecia ~ "Doing the little things for each other is one of the best and most rewarding things to keep a marriage going."*

82. *Debbie (**bonus**) ~ "Marry someone who is kind to animals! A kind heart goes a long way."*

83. *Jeremy ~ "Don't do drugs."*

84. *Edwin ~ "Remember your anniversaries!"*

85. *Nadine (**bonus**) ~ "Love each other just as the word of God says to do, remember your one body now, you can't be mad at yourself forever!"*

86. *Kevin ~ "Be prepared to give as well as get."*

87. *Laura Faye (**bonus**) ~ "Always see it from the others perspective. You do not have to agree, but if you can understand and respect, that's the key!"*

88. *Tosh (**bonus**) ~ "Continue to date."*

89. *Deon (**bonus**) ~ "Consult God before making a decision."*

90. *Pastor Raymond (**bonus**) ~ Men we are to be providers of our home. But I learned that this is not limited to only monetary provision. We must provide whatever is lacking in the home.*

91. *Tangela (**bonus**) ~ "Love against the world...because it will come for you and there will be times that you only have each other."*

92. *Octavia (**bonus**) ~ "Remember no one is perfect and romance novels are fiction. Love the real person for both good and bad."*

93. *Mario (**bonus**) ~ "You have instincts for a reason, trust them."*

94. *Derek (**bonus**) ~ "Keep updated on your spouse's love language (hugs, kisses, sex, verbal affirmations, money/gifts, etc.). The language he/she had at the beginning may not be the same year after year."*

95. *Dezetta (**bonus**) ~ "Don't EVER stop dating your spouse!"*

96. Paula (**bonus**) ~ *"In some situations, silence is not golden. You cannot fix what you won't confront. I've had to face that in my own life because I would avoid confrontation at all costs, however; there is a way to say what is needed and still respect the other person."*

97. Brenda (**bonus**) ~ *"Talk out what is bothering you. If not, cheating may become your reality because you may start confiding in another instead of your spouse."*

98. Charmion (**bonus**) ~ *"Actions speak louder than words. Always show love. It goes much farther than just saying it."*

99. Sophia (**bonus**) ~ *"Remember, your spouse is not perfect and neither are you!"*

100. Karen (**bonus**) ~ *"Don't take one another for granted."*

101. Brittany (**bonus**) ~ *"Read The Power of a Praying Husband/Wife book by Stormie Omartian!! These collections of prayers will change your heart INSTANTLY!"*

Endnotes

1. Strange but True Facts, http://stangebuttru. blogspot.com/2012/11/strange-but-true-facts-about-marriage.html, accessed August 25, 2014.

2. Random Facts, http://facts.randomhistory. com/divorce-facts.html, accessed August 25, 2014.

3. The Blog, http://www.huffingtonpost.com/meg-conley/five-reasons-you-should-h_b_5647291. html, accessed August 25, 2014.

4. *God's Little Devotional Book for Couples*, Honor books, Inc., Tulsa, Oklahoma, 1995.

5. Morris, Robert: *The Blessed Life*. Ventura, California, 2002.

www.ingramcontent.com/pod-product-compliance
Lightning Source LLC
Chambersburg PA
CBHW070758100426
42742CB00012B/2186